Helping People Addicted to Methamphetamine

Helping People Addicted to Methamphetamine

A Creative New Approach for Families and Communities

NICOLAS T. TAYLOR AND
HERBERT C. COVEY

Westport, Connecticut
London

Library of Congress Cataloging-in-Publication Data

Taylor, Nicolas T., 1965–
   Helping people addicted to methamphetamine : a creative new approach for families
   and communities / Nicolas T. Taylor and Herbert C. Covey.
     p. cm.
   Includes bibliographical references and index.
   ISBN 978–0–275–99908–7 (alk. paper)
1. Methamphetamine abuse. I. Covey, Herbert C. II. Title.
RC568.A45.T39 2008
616.86′4—dc22   2008023811

British Library Cataloguing in Publication Data is available.

Library of Congress Catalog Card Number: 2008023811
ISBN: 978–0–275–99908–7

First published in 2008

Praeger Publishers, 88 Post Road West, Westport, CT 06881
An imprint of Greenwood Publishing Group, Inc.
www.praeger.com

Printed in the United States of America

The paper used in this book complies with the
Permanent Paper Standard issued by the National
Information Standards Organization (Z39.48–1984).

10 9 8 7 6 5 4 3 2 1

This book is dedicated to the families, friends, parents, children, treatment providers, judges, teachers, counselors, law enforcement officers, employers, members of faith-based organizations, elected officials, and communities that care enough about those addicted to methamphetamine to take positive action. We also want to acknowledge our families and especially our spouses Teresha Taylor and Marty Covey who supported us throughout this endeavor. Special thanks to Marty Covey, who provided editorial suggestions and helped greatly in writing this book. Her contribution was immense. Thanks also to Senior Editor Debbie Carvalko of Praeger Publishers, who provided excellent guidance and displayed great patience with the authors. She has been a valuable partner in seeing this book come to fruition.

Contents

Preface

Methamphetamine has impacted families and communities in such a way that for the past 10 years treatment programs and judicial systems have struggled with how to intervene and to provide the right kind of rehabilitative help. While not entirely different from other substances of abuse, meth is unique enough to challenge these systems to come up with the most effective ways of helping people not only stop using the drug but also stop hanging around other people who continue to use it. At one point the most devastating cases of communities being impacted by meth were limited to the western regions of the nation. That has changed, and with the exception of only the eastern seaboard states, really, meth has penetrated every community, both urban and rural, and has crossed almost all ethno- and demographic boundaries.

Treatment for meth addiction must involve the broad sober community in which the addict lives; otherwise it becomes almost impossible for people who are trying to stop using meth to separate themselves from groups of people who use it. What this book provides is the description of a creative new approach to treating meth addiction that can be used to guide a true community-based intervention. The key to this intervention is the practice of carving out a niche within the sober community so that people recovering from meth have a place to go as well as the necessary support to break ties with other meth users.

Families and community leaders are invited to consider the principles and practices described in the pages of this book as they develop treatment plans and strategies for individual people addicted to meth as well as broad groups of people accessed through social service and judicial referral systems. We know for certain that there is neither a magic potion nor a silver bullet that could be used to help every addict. Instead, there are general principles of practice that stem from an informed awareness of those things that make meth unique. It is those principles that we have attempted to present in this book as part of our general treatment approach. In this way, we hope to help enhance what is being attempted by people who generally care to see people addicted to meth move toward living a sober lifestyle.

We are often asked why we would focus so much energy on the treatment of addiction to just one substance of abuse when there are literally millions of other people around the nation who either struggle with addiction to different chemicals, other than meth, or are family members of people addicted to other drugs. The answer to this question is twofold. First, people addicted to meth present as a unique challenge to treatment systems because of the detrimental effects associated with meth, specifically. This uniqueness does necessitate consideration of a treatment approach for meth. Second, the true community-based intervention we have attempted to describe, while effective in treating meth addiction, introduces creative new treatment concepts that can be employed by families and communities for the treatment of other substances of abuse as well.

Very little that is good has come from the widespread use of meth across this nation. However, if we consider what the impact of meth has done to improve the treatment systems and practices of communities hardest hit by meth, we may see that dealing with so many people addicted to meth has helped us to improve how we prevent meth use and how we treat as communities those addicted to it.

CHAPTER 1

Introduction

THE METH EPIDEMIC

Drug epidemics are not new to the United States. The abuse of patent medicines around the turn of the 20th century is estimated to have affected more than a million Americans when it was at its peak. When it was discovered that the primary "curative agents" in these snake-oil-type medications were highly addictive chemicals, such as heroin and cocaine, the Pure Food and Drug Act was passed in 1906. This law required drug companies to indicate on the labels of all medicines the exact nature and amounts of addictive substances found in their products (Hanson, Venturelli, and Fleckenstein 2004).

Alcohol, although sometimes not considered a drug, was at the center of a very unique epidemic during the period of prohibition. The use of alcohol among the general population appears to have declined during this period of American history. However, the illegal production and distribution of alcohol by moonshiners and bootleggers and its sale in underground bars, known as speakeasies, spread across the nation and spurred violence between law enforcement and organized crime. Police corruption, violence, and the growth of organized crime were the primary reasons prohibition was repealed in 1933 (Hanson, Venturelli, and Fleckenstein 2004).

Other drugs, including heroin in the 1930s, hallucinogens in the 1960s, and crack cocaine in the 1980s, have all been described as reaching epidemic-like proportions during periods of highest use. Then there is meth.

An epidemic is defined as a rapid spread or increase in the occurrence of something. Epidemics are typically thought of as a temporary prevalence;

a wave of occurrence, if you will, that seems to have an onset, a peak, and then a period of recovery. The use of methamphetamine throughout the United States, and especially in the midwestern and western states, first started getting the attention of law enforcement, treatment providers, and public policy makers in the late 1980s and the early 1990s. Even at that time, there was talk in these circles that the way the drug seemed to be affecting people and the numbers of new users from small communities suggested the start of an epidemic. By the mid-1990s, there really was no denying the issue. It seemed that this illegally manufactured drug was taking over the lives of the people who started using it and they did not seem to be getting much better, even with strong legal consequences, having children taken away, and negative effects on their appearance, health, and general lifestyle.

Meth quickly became known as the "walk-away drug" because people who used it seemed to walk away not only from their families, jobs, and responsibilities but also from other drugs of abuse. Once individuals started using meth, it seemed to take over their lives. They may use other drugs, but these other drugs were often either to prepare for or enhance the effects of meth or to help recover from the use of it.

Time magazine in a 1998 article followed a group of meth users in Billings, Montana and documented some of the unique characteristics of the people who use the drug and of the meth-using culture. The article referred to the new "crank epidemic," and pretty much from that time on, the floodgates were opened for popular media; governmental publications, too, referred to the rising meth epidemic. People believed that because this was an epidemic and since all epidemics are only temporary increases in the prevalence of something, meth would eventually reach its peak and decline. This decline would occur, they reasoned, because it was so detrimental to the health and well-being of users. After meth diminished, the U.S. population could then begin bracing itself for whatever drug du jour would be coming next.

It has now been more than 10 years since meth use in the United States was first popularly labeled an epidemic. Every indicator of prevalence seems to suggest that we are nowhere near the climax. In fact, if anything, the trend still seems to be rising. Treatment admissions for people addicted to meth, arrests for use or possession of the drug, the numbers of people testing positive for meth at the time of arrest for any crime, the numbers of children removed from the care of meth-using parents, hospital discharges for medical problems associated with meth use, emergency room admissions for meth intoxication, and coroner reports for meth-related fatalities have all been on the rise and seem to show no sign of leveling off. Meth, once thought of as primarily a rural western/midwestern drug, has made its way across the Mississippi river and is even beginning to show signs of increased use in the eastern seaboard states, where it has always been thought it could never supplant the drugs of choice in those regions, such as heroin and crack cocaine.

While meth has always seemed to have been used by a greater proportion of women compared to other drugs, it was thought to have some racial, ethnic, and cultural boundaries that it did not frequently cross. Once labeled "red-neck heroin" and "poor man's cocaine," meth was thought to be primarily the drug of choice of people pejoratively called "white trash," apropos its widespread use among predominantly poor Caucasian populations. Now it seems to have spread into other populations as well. Those hardest hit include not only poor Caucasian men and women but also Native Americans living on reservations, Alaskan Natives, homosexual men from all parts of the country, Hispanic men and women from the Southwest, people from Hawaii and the pacific island nations, and Asians. Perhaps the only major ethnic group that has not yet experienced an increase in meth use to any great extent is the African American population, but that may change as meth becomes more widespread in the southern and eastern states, which have a much higher percentage of African Americans.

Traditionally, meth use has been highest among adults ages 20 to 40. A collective sigh of relief was breathed nationwide when it appeared that meth use was actually declining among adolescent populations. Then, however, it was noted that the surveys being used to measure drug use trends among teenagers were administered primarily through school systems. Since, presumably, teens who use meth are not likely to still be in school, these estimates of decreased use among teenagers are probably hopeful, but not totally accurate. This seems to be the case, especially since anecdotal evidence actually suggests more teenagers are trying meth and are becoming addicted. Furthermore, when interviewed most meth users report that their initial use began sometime during their teenage years.

The use of meth in the United States seems to have endured longer than was expected and it seems to have impacted more people than was anticipated. Because of the geographic spread of meth, some authors have started referring to its use across the nation as a pandemic, meaning that it is an epidemic that has spread over a large area. However, as was mentioned, the spread of meth has not just been to new states and regions. It has also crossed into populations, cultures, and communities not previously affected by it. Because of this, the transitory nature of the meth epidemic is questionable. Perhaps a new epidemiologic term can be invented just for meth. Maybe that term should be metapandemic, or even methapandemic.

SOLUTIONS?

The most logical step to begin addressing the "methapandemic" is prevention. It really makes no sense trying to address a problem until we figure out a way to keep the problem from escalating in the first place. Prevention means to intervene, to keep those who have never tried meth from even trying it once. It also means working to keep those who have tried meth from using it again. However, unless prevention efforts start before a problem has really grown into anything significant, they do nothing about existing cases. While prevention is important to keep the meth epidemic from becoming even bigger and affecting even more people and communities, the real solution lies in knowing how to help the millions of people already addicted to meth.

While only about 60,000 people are admitted each year to substance abuse treatment centers for methamphetamine addiction, approximately 12.5 million Americans, ages 12 and over, report having tried meth sometime during their life. About 3 million report having used meth in the past year, and about 900,000 admit to having used it sometime during the past month (SAMHSA 2005a). While recent use is not necessarily an indication of a severe meth abuse problem, if it is conservatively assumed that half of the approximately 900,000 people who admitted to having used meth in the past month are addicted and need treatment, then current treatment admission suggests that less than 15 percent of them actually end up engaging in treatment. Of this small percentage who do wind up in treatment, even fewer take maximum advantage of the treatment they do receive by establishing and maintaining long-term abstinence from the drug.

So, is there any hope? For families and communities whose lives have been touched personally by people who have become addicted to meth, hope can be hard to come by. The high rate of relapse and the difficulty of getting someone addicted to meth to go to treatment in the first place make the idea of long-term recovery seem unlikely and bleak. The situation is not helped at all by false and sensationalized reports in the media of people who "once they become addicted to meth are hooked for life" and the false claim that less than 6 percent of people who ever use meth recover.

This book is not intended to build up false hope among people whose lives have been devastated by meth either because they use the drug or because they are close to someone who uses it. However, to suggest that people cannot recover from meth use or that it is so difficult that almost no one is able to stop doing it once they have started is a tremendous disservice and dishonor to the thousands of people who have been able to successfully stop using meth after becoming severely addicted. There do seem to be many people who are using meth, and that number does seem to be increasing. But the "chicken little" type hysteria about the ravages of meth throughout the nation does not bring us any closer to a solution either. What this book does provide is a factually based, honest appraisal of what meth is and what it really takes for someone to stop using it. In that way, this book could really be considered a treatment manual since a theory for meth addiction is posited and then, based on this theory, a community-based approach for treating meth addiction is described.

However, this is not a treatment manual in that it is not written for treatment professionals specifically. Instead, it is intended for communities and families dealing with meth addiction. So much of what makes meth such a unique drug has to do with the distasteful subculture associated with people who use meth. Meth truly is a community drug, and it requires community solutions. The motivation and desire for sobriety of the addicted individual is, of course, paramount. But there is much that can and must be done by sober communities throughout the country to assist with treatment. Communities can help the increasing numbers of people who are becoming addicted to meth have what it takes to stop using the drug and to distance themselves from other people who do use it.

This book describes how communities and families can participate in the treatment of people addicted to meth in a way that truly addresses the reasons why meth is so addicting and why people continue to use it in spite of the fact that it causes them such serious problems. A traditional view of treatment is that it is something provided by a trained professional, often while the addicted person is out of the community, and in an inpatient, residential, or hospital-based rehabilitation program. While removal from the community is sometimes required for treatment to be most effective, especially in the beginning stages of recovery, it is our position that treatment is most effective when it is accomplished while the addicted person is living in their home community. Even for people whose severe addiction requires that they begin their treatment with a medically monitored detoxification or a structured inpatient experience, they will still need a successful outpatient treatment experience at some point if they are going to someday be successful at remaining sober while living in their home community, wherever that might be.

A well-trained competent substance abuse treatment provider is an indispensable part of the treatment a meth-addicted person needs to receive. However, families and communities have traditionally been relegated to the role of adjunct participants in the therapy, and there often is little guarantee they will be involved in the therapy, if at all. This is a critical flaw when it comes to treatment of meth addiction. With other substances of abuse or psychological disorders, it may be the case that the primary vehicle for the treatment is the exclusive, private, confidential, and personal relationship with a trusted therapist. However, with meth addiction, important as the relationship with the therapist might be, it is really the client's relationship with their community that requires the greatest focus.

This is partially because addicted individuals have most likely distanced themselves almost to the point of complete exclusion from their sober communities but also because people addicted to meth have little hope of living soberly without this important source of support. Involvement of family and the community in outpatient treatment is also critical because an important part of treatment, as will be explained later in this book, is helping the addicted individual get to the point at which the person can feel pleasure because of things that are naturally pleasurable as opposed to using meth to feel good. These "pleasure recalibration exercises" require the involvement of family and community members to be most effective. The inherent difficulty of this kind of work lies in the fact that many people addicted to meth may not have ever even learned to associate feelings of pleasure with events, situations, people, or objects that are naturally pleasurable, such as fun activities with family members or engaging experiences with sober friends. This may be because from an early age, they begin associating good feelings or the removal of bad feelings primarily through the use of drugs and alcohol from their own use or because that was what was modeled for them by other people in their lives.

Community-based efforts are not new solutions to social problems. The tragic Columbine school shooting in 1999 and other acts of violence on school campuses have forced law enforcement, school officials, mental health professionals, students, and families to work together to determine effective prevention and interdiction efforts. The issue is simply too broad and complex to be effectively dealt with by one community agency or entity. Helping people who are addicted to meth is no different. The demands of the treatment effort are often so involved that it is really more than any one individual, one family, or one agency can provide. For this reason, perhaps more than a guide to meth recovery, this book is designed to provide families and community treatment teams with needed strategies and collective approaches to maximize the effectiveness of their efforts to help people stop using meth.

In discussing strategies and techniques, theories, and practices to effectively help people stop using meth, it is important to not lose sight of the individuals whose lives have been ruined by the drug. A community-based approach to treating meth addiction assumes that the addicted individual has been, and can once again be, a valued community member. As community members, their individual stories and circumstances are important to consider. For this reason, we will begin with two stories of people who have experienced extreme addiction to meth. The stories are not just about the people but also about their families and communities who were impacted by their addiction as well.

The first is the story of Sasha. It is a true story in that it is made up of bits and pieces of several real stories we have become aware of over the last 10 years that we have been working closely with people addicted to meth. The conclusion of the story, however, is the actual account of what happened to a young woman we had seen professionally, whom Sasha most resembles. It is in her memory and in the hope of helping other addicts and their families that this work is dedicated. Chris's story is that of a real and truly courageous individual who has now become a beacon of hope for people addicted to meth and for families and communities trying to help them. This work is also dedicated to his life and to helping others find what he has found.

CHAPTER 2

Two Meth Stories and the Important Role of Community

Case histories can teach us important lessons about meth use and how family and community dynamics can play out. The following are two case histories of meth use and the role it plays in the lives of users, family members, friends, and those trying to serve them. The names of the individuals have been changed to protect identities. The stories shed light on some of the patterns found with meth use and the struggles of overcoming this drug. The first story is that of Sasha and the second, of Chris.

SASHA'S STORY

Sasha was a vivacious, fun-loving 15-year-old who used her good looks and outgoing personality to get whatever she wanted. She loved adventure and was not afraid to seek out those in her world who could provide her with excitement. She was skilled at using her charm to get whatever she wanted from people, especially her father. She had her father wrapped tightly around her little finger and he would do anything she wanted to keep her happy.

Her father had emigrated from another country and quickly opened a small business in town. He soon met and married her mother, whose family had grown up in the region. Her mother and generations of family members had a long history of alcohol dependency.

Sasha became involved with meth through her friend Kim, who was 13 years old at the time. Both had used their good looks to gain admission to local adult parties with people who were two to three times older than them. The older adults at these parties supplied them with meth. These same adults, almost always male, promised to look after them and make sure no one gave the two bad meth or took advantage of them when they were high or crashing. To free up time for these numerous parties and to keep their parents from becoming suspicious, both girls told their parents they were going to each other's houses to do school work.

Sasha first entered a substance abuse treatment outpatient clinic, following her placement in a group home by child protection. Child protection had placed her in a group home, following an incident between her father and her 33-year-old boyfriend. Her father became suspicious, from the amount of time Sasha was "spending" on school work. He also received a call from the school indicating that Sasha was performing poorly in school. Equipped with this information, he decided to investigate how she was really spending her time. He began to secretly follow her around town. On one of these occasions, he was shocked to see her hanging around with an older man whom he did not know. This man was Sasha's boyfriend and meth supplier. On impulse, he confronted the couple and asked Sasha to come home with him. She refused, which only angered him more. She in turn was angry at him for following, not trusting, and catching her lying. The situation became more intense when he forced her into his car while she was high on meth. During the struggle, he slapped her hard across the face, and upon seeing this, neighbors called the police, who arrested him. He would later be convicted of assault on a child and harassment.

The police found marks on Sasha's face and drug paraphernalia in her purse. They also searched the boyfriend's car and found nothing. As a result of this incident, child protection was contacted, and Sasha was placed in a group home. As part of this placement, Sasha was required to go to drug treatment.

From the beginning, Sasha's treatment did not go well. She resisted every attempt by anyone to help her with her addiction. To Sasha, the real demon was her father, who she insisted had been abusive to her. She sat through treatment groups and therapy but mostly was disruptive and failed to get anything out of the efforts to help her. Her treatment did not last long, as she ran away from her group home. Her caseworker and parents did not know where she was living but suspected that she was staying with the boyfriend. Eventually, Sasha came home and promised that she would never use meth again or associate with people who did.

A New Beginning?

Everything went well for about six months, and her father was the happiest he had ever been. Her mother even cut back on drinking. Her father concluded that Sasha's meth use and relationships with other users were a passing fancy that she had outgrown. Over the first three months, she basically stayed home, watched television, and felt depressed. During this time, she believed her feelings were similar to her mother's and thought she now understood why her mother drank all the time. On the surface, everything seemed to be on the right path with Sasha. Her parents believed her meth use was in the past, and a bright future lay ahead.

Although things were going well, Sasha was bored and wanted to go back to school. The plan had been to keep her inside the house and away from school to avoid her being spotted by the child protection worker. After three months of Sasha's lobbying, her parents agreed she could go back to school. Initially, she started off going to school and doing well. Soon child protection contacted the family and decided that because she was doing well in school and the home seemed to be stable, Sasha could remain at home and continue in school.

All this worked well for about a year although Sasha picked up a few under-age drinking tickets. Her parents thought that at least she was not involved with meth anymore. They were also not too upset when she was arrested for shoplifting while with her friend Kim. About half way through her junior year, she dropped out of high school and lied to her parents by telling them she was getting credit through a work-study program. Her parents, desperate to believe Sasha, did not follow up on these claims. What they did see was their daughter seemed to have money and assumed that this must be from her work study. What they did not know was her 34-year-old boyfriend was released from prison and was back in the picture. He was supplying her meth, and she had simply been waiting for him to come back into her life.

The thought of his daughter's being back in the meth scene was so unacceptable and unimaginable that her father avoided asking questions. Although he knew well the signs of meth use that were surfacing with Sasha, he put them out of his mind. Eventually, her behavior became so obvious he decided to act. He developed a pattern of staying up at night waiting to confront her when she came home. These confrontations discouraged her, so she simply quit coming home. He then began, as he had in the past, following her around town. He discovered that she was once again spending time with older strangers.

On one occasion, he followed her to a building and in a moment of anger went into the building carrying a baseball bat to take care of the situation and get his daughter away from this drug-using group. In a rage, he took matters in his own hands and entered the apartment, demanding to see his daughter. No one cooperated, and he swung his bat at the people he believed were the meth addicts who got his daughter involved with meth again. During his outburst, he searched through the rooms and encountered other young girls similar to his daughter. Finally, he found her in the bathroom crouched on the floor next to the toilet with a hypodermic needle in her arm. She was crying and did not bother to look but pushed the contents of the needle into her arm. This was the first time that he had seen anyone inject drugs, let alone his own daughter. He then took her to his car and brought her home.

ANOTHER ATTEMPT AT TREATMENT

A few days later, after the effects of the meth wore off, her parents took her to an outpatient clinic. They hoped to find a residential treatment program for her that would be located out of town. The therapist suggested that this would only be a short-term solution and that when she was released, she would simply return to the same meth-using community. They disagreed and thought that if they could just get her away from the meth-using community, Sasha would forget these people and be able to stay off meth. They decided that a year-round vacation bible camp located across the state was the best place for her.

While getting away from the meth crowd was a good move, the bible camp did not provide substance abuse evaluations that would have revealed how much she used, why she used it, and the number and types of drugs she used. In addition, the camp provided no individual or group counseling, discussions about the harm caused by drug use, basic life skills training, nor mental health assistance. Most important, the camp offered no planning for structure or accountability. Her parents did not care at the time; they just wanted her someplace, safe and away. They would worry about aftercare when she came home.

Similar to her patterns, initially Sasha did well and seemed once again to be on the right path. She was bored but complying. However, three months into her stay her boyfriend and Kim decided to visit her. When they arrived, they told camp officials that they just wanted to take her on a day trip. They picked her up and never returned. After two days, the camp officials contacted her parents and let them know she was missing. Her parents understandably were angry at the camp and began to painfully search for Sasha. She was back in town and very aware that her parents were looking for her.

More Loss of Contact with Her Family

Sasha had very little contact with her parents over the next few years. They would occasionally see each other but exchanges were brief and superficial. They noticed her appearance changed as she lost weight, had wrinkles, had yellowed teeth, developed open sores, and added several tattoos.

During this time, Sasha's boyfriend continued his criminal lifestyle. He eventually was arrested for a series of crimes. She also was involved and faced jail time. She spent about a week in jail but was released on bond after telling the judge she was going to live with her parents. She also told her parents she was angry with the boyfriend and that she never wanted to see him again. Her parents fell for her story and viewed her as a victim of forces beyond her control. She also told them she was pregnant.

At Sasha's trial, the judge sentenced her to a residential drug treatment program. She enrolled in an outpatient program, which had special track for pregnant women. It was an exciting new beginning for Sasha and her parents. Soon she would give birth to a baby girl. The baby would become the focus, rather than Sasha's need to address her addiction to meth. Eventually, she left the program to live with her parents, and upon hearing this, the judge sentenced Sasha to six months of jail.

Sasha's jail sentence did little to help her or her parents. When she finished her sentence, she started staying out late and soon became involved with her same old meth-using friends. Her father was the first to recognize the signs of her meth use but, after all of these false starts, did not know what to do. He disengaged and stayed away from home by working long hours. His working made him feel like he was at least doing something with all the bills and expenses for his family.

Toward the End

Sasha started spending more time away than at home. Her parents focused on the baby and avoided thinking about what was going on with their daughter. Sasha, to those who saw her, looked increasingly terrible. She was deeply into meth again. She told her substance abuse counselor that her life was out of control, a message she shared with anyone who would listen. Her counselor noticed she had cuts on her arms which corresponded with her references to suicide. She indicated that when she was not using meth, she felt severely depressed and suicidal. She shared that unless someone forced her to quit, she was not sure she could stop. She was afraid that if she stopped using, she would kill herself.

Two weeks after the counselor had seen Sasha, he received a call from the county coroner who wanted to subpoena his records on a female patient to rule out whether or not her death by drug overdose was suicide. That patient was Sasha. Apparently, she had taken an overdose of prescription narcotics after being up for four days using meth. Right after she had taken the pills, Sasha came home to her parents and admitted to them that she had been using meth heavily. She told them she was home now and ready to stop. She had asked if she could hold her baby daughter who was sleeping at the time. She held her and was crying softly as the baby slept. Sasha started to look very tired so her mother took the baby from her and told her that she should go to bed. Sasha said nothing about the pills she had taken, kissed the baby, and then told her mom that this time she thought she would finally be able to stop. She told her she loved her and then she went to bed. Her mother did not say anything. Her father found her dead in the morning.

CHRIS'S STORY

The second case history is that of Chris. Chris's story differs from Sasha's in many respects but also shares some common themes. Chris grew up as the second son of a middle-class family in Southern California. Chris certainly enjoyed a fairly stable childhood and early adolescence. While in high school, he was a popular young man and played the high school basketball team. Chris had always felt that he was a little different from his older siblings in that he was a little more rowdy and a little more likely to get himself into trouble. It was during high school that Chris first began experimenting with drugs and alcohol. At first, he was mainly involved in drinking with high school friends, but then that quickly became regular consumption of marijuana and then occasional use of cocaine. Chris's cocaine use at first was primarily social in that he would only use it at parties and with friends. However, as the use of cocaine became more and more appealing to him, he eventually reached the point of using it alone and seeking the drug by himself.

Chris passed through several years of difficult work and educational experiences, most of which failed because of his excessive drug and alcohol use. Aware of these issues, his parents moved to Arizona to help Chris distance himself from his drug-using friends. He called this move across country a "geographic treatment." But no matter where he lived, he knew drugs would be available.

After the move, Chris found a job outside town. At this job, Chris's coworkers introduced him to meth. He had heard about "speed" and thought it was harmless and easy to manage. As is true with most people who become addicted to meth, Chris first met and became involved with other people who used meth before he started using it. Virtually all of his coworkers, including his boss, used meth. On the job, he saw what it did for them and decided to try it out. He had used stimulants before and immediately found meth appealing. When the job was completed and before they moved to the next location, Chris's coworkers made sure that he was connected with the supplier to guarantee he had continued access to meth.

Seeing how much energy he had, and his good attitude, Chris's parents started having him work in the family store part-time. They did not realize that much of what they were seeing was due to his meth use. His mood seemed very positive, and he seemed to be excited about life and about what he was doing. Eventually, his mother and father began to trust him more and more and gave him management responsibilities. This spelled disaster for Chris because it gave him ready and easy access to chemicals to make meth.

Chris started hanging out at bars and began to make friends with people who used meth. He believed the drug actually helped him to go out at night, hang out in bars, drink, and then make it to work on time in the morning. But like any drug, it began to take more than it gave. Eventually, he started missing days of work. He began to cross personal boundaries, such as paying his bills on time. When not high, Chris experienced severe depression and anger but still believed that meth was good for him. He also changed emotionally, and when he was not high, he was incredibly depressed and angry. If there is one emotion that overrode all the others, it was his anger.

Chris thought that this time in his life "meth worked for him." He liked being able to stay up all night doing what he wanted to do and then still being able to make it to work the next day and have enough energy to work through the entire day. Chris was using a quarter to half of a gram per week for about $20 a quarter. It was relatively cheap and kept him high for hours. As his use continued, he eventually developed a tolerance for the drug and needed more and more of it to maintain a high and the desired effects. It was about this time that Chris first started thinking about selling meth and, eventually, bought a quarter pound of meth. With this large amount, he began dealing to a small community of people.

A MISDIAGNOSIS AND ATTEMPT TO HELP

Prolonged heavy involvement with meth leads to a violent lifestyle. Chris was no exception. He scared people and sometimes acted on his increasingly violent disposition. Well aware of his frequent and often violent mood swings, Chris's parents remained unaware of his heavy meth use. They speculated that he would benefit from seeing a psychologist. His parents wondered if Chris was suffering from clinical depression and they made arrangements for him to have a psychological assessment.

Chris saw a psychologist, but of course he did not tell him about his meth use. Instead, he talked about his depression and lack of energy. It was obvious to the psychologist that Chris was depressed. Chris's experience both with his parents and with the psychologist around the issue of a psychological disorder raises a very important point about the interface of meth addiction with psychiatric or behavioral health diagnoses, treatment, and services. Mental health treatment is driven by the self-reporting of symptoms and level of functioning. In some cases, collateral contacts, such as family members, may offer their observations as well. However, nothing is ever discovered about substance abuse, meth use specifically, unless the individual reports it, or unless people familiar with the client report it to the clinician. Subsequently, hidden addiction is often mistaken for many different kinds of psychological disorders. This is mainly because the effects of meth look similar to symptoms associated with particular psychopathologies, such as schizophrenia, bipolar mood disorder, major depressive, episode-recurrent adjustment disorder with mixed disturbance of conduct and emotions, and ADHD (attention deficit/hyperactivity disorder).

The psychologist also diagnosed him with adult ADHD and made arrangements for Chris to begin taking 10 mg a day of methylphenidate (Ritalin). Chris filled the prescription for Ritalin and then promptly sold it to other meth addicts. Many meth users are master manipulators of others to maintain a steady stream of the drug for personal use. In this vein, Chris manipulated a mental health diagnosis and corresponding prescription to influence family members and his therapist. All of these manipulations hid his addiction and allowed him to continue to maintain his meth-using lifestyle.

The requirement for patients to receive some kind of drug use monitoring before receiving prescriptions for psychotropic medications makes good sense but is infrequently done. As a result, too often the symptoms of substance abuse are misinterpreted as signs of a psychological disturbance and treatment then proceeds although there may be a volatile mismatch between the treatment being delivered and the drug users' lifestyle or functioning. This can be seen in Chris's case, as he took the prescription for Ritalin and sold the medication to other addicts.

CHRIS LEARNS HOW TO MAKE METH

As Chris's use of meth progressed, so did his criminal involvement in the distribution and sale of meth. The next step for Chris was for him to begin making meth. He had tried to make it on many occasions but had not been successful. It is well known that meth is easy to make, and there are numerous recipes available in books and on the Internet. It is even easier when you have an experienced cook show you how to do it. Chris, after some experimentation and failures, decided to get some help from a meth cook and eventually mastered the process.

That was the beginning of Chris's most significant involvement in the subculture of meth addiction; that of being a meth cook. Cooking meth, for Chris, was just as addicting as using it. He found that being a meth cook gave him high status in the meth-using community and allowed him to meet his needs for the drug. For the next months of his life, Chris was lost in a crazy vortex of chaos, meth cooking, meth use, violence, sex, and paranoia. Chris used his parents' business to get regular supplies of the chemicals he needed to make meth. He lied and stole whatever he needed from his family and his parents' business to support his cooking and his meth addiction. Eventually, Chris started running into problems because he started using more and more of the meth he was making and selling less of it.

Trust became kind of a difficult animal for Chris. He lost the trust of his family, and then at the same time, his meth use made it difficult for him to trust anyone. He became increasingly paranoid. Chris became concerned about people wanting to steal drugs from him, about people he thought were going to turn him in, and about strangers he thought were calling him just so that they could get drugs from him. Chris also moved rapidly in and out of relationships. He would often meet women, impulsively live with them, and then within two or three days become paranoid about their turning him in or stealing from him.

Time and again, Chris had seen fellow meth addicts who were incredibly skillful at keeping their meth use and distribution hidden from the police get arrested and found out because they had an argument or domestic disturbance with their spouse or romantic partner. Chris stayed away from relationships because he did not want to get injured or to hurt someone else. Mostly, he just did not, in his own words, "want to get caught." Chris eventually became so paranoid and erratic, especially about women who were calling his house.

Chris's home became completely toxic. There was yellow iodine running down the walls of his home. He would spend hours and hours painting his house just to try and cover up the iodine. He did not develop some of the normal signs of heavy meth use, such as hair loss and dental problems; and he never picked at his skin. He did develop severe blisters and sores on his feet, especially when he was cooking. This was because he would be on his feet for all hours of the day and night for several days and nights in a row.

Chris Gets Arrested and the Path to Sobriety

Chris continued to cook meth, even knowing that he was being investigated by law enforcement agents, and was arrested. Up until that night, he had never spent more than 2 or 3 hours in jail, and that had been 20 years ago. Chris's experience in jail was not unlike that of other people arrested on serious drug charges. He was terrified about what was going to happen to him and angry at his family and others that they were not doing more to bail him out.

Chris found his county jail time to be frightening. He was unsure of what might happen, and he wanted out. Chris had attempted to get his parents to agree to allow him to be released into their custody, but they refused. When Chris did have the chance to speak with his father, he told him that he was in the place that he had chosen for himself.

While in jail, Chris went to his first 12-step meeting. There, he was the only one who cried and shared his feelings. He also attended a Bible study group and started to feel connected to God. Chris later shared that he began to see God working in the lives of the other guys in his pod. He also discovered that he took much for granted and began to focus on the little things in life. He started to see God in the little things.

During his attempts to get out of jail, Chris hoped his parents would allow him to be released to their home. He called them, and his dad answered the phone and indicated he would not bond Chris out of jail. Chris argued with him over why they were not getting him out. Instead, his father reminded him of a friend who might be an option. Chris called the friend, and he agreed to let him move in after he had bonded out.

The Redemptive Community

Chris was released from jail. His friend and his friend's wife came to court, and the judge released him to their custody. His parents also had shown up at court that day and were there to greet him when he was released from jail. He sat on the street curb and cried because he could not believe he was released.

The next morning his friend took him over to another friend's house. Before he did, he told Chris something he would never forget, that his recovery would be based on the type of community Chris created around himself. Chris visited their friend's home every day the first week he was out of jail. Chris's friend took him to numerous homes and have Chris tell his story of where he had been. Chris always experienced a sense of acceptance. While staying with his friend, Chris was responsible for things around the house, weeding, painting, and sheetrocking.

Everything was on the right path. However, his change was not completely without incident. Shortly after he was released from jail and while he was still living with his friends, they had to leave town, and they left Chris in their home alone for several days. The freedom was a little too much for Chris to handle in these early stages of his recovery. Almost as if it were a reflex, Chris went to various drug stores and bought medications that contained ephedrine. He started soaking the pills in a solvent to pull out the pure ephedrine as he had done so often before. The difference this time was that in the midst of starting the process of making meth, he realized what he was doing and thought of everything he had fought so hard to regain and would lose if he started using meth again. These thoughts were strong enough, as was his resolve not to let down his new sober support group, to stop himself from going any further with the cook. He ended up flushing the pills and the solvent down the toilet. The experience scared him, but it also gave him a new sense of competency regarding his ability to actually do what he would need to do to be able to maintain a sober lifestyle.

One day as Chris was at his parents' store, he ran into an old friend. The friend was angry because Chris's parents told him what had happened. The friend took Chris to his first 12-step meeting outside jail. Chris felt a sense of acceptance in that meeting. After that meeting, people gave him their phone numbers, invited Chris out to lunch, and acted like they really wanted to be around him. Chris started going to 12-step meetings regularly, even twice a day on occasion. Chris also worked out five days a week, which he thought was important to his recovery, self-image, and getting healthy, both physically and mentally. Chris began to eat homemade meals, and eat right. He also started taking vitamins. It had been a long time since Chris had taken good care of himself.

At a 12-step meeting, Chris met a person who agreed to be his sponsor. His sponsor was pretty close to Chris's age and had been a former athlete, so they liked to work out five days a week. They became buddies and began reading together the *Big Book* and the *Twelve in Twelve*. His sponsor was going through a divorce, and did not have a job or car. So both helped each other out, and Chris had a car. They went to meetings and fellowship together. They completed the 12-steps within about 6 months, and then Chris started looking for some other type of spiritual growth. He believed that spiritual growth was the key to his recovery.

The only aspect of his treatment that Chris remembered was the first step he took at the end of a session, and a day of psychodrama. Treatment was just something he did, but recovery was something Chris lived. He participated in an aftercare program that lasted about two months. Again, there was not a lot he remembered. He did not need treatment but love and support. Now he was getting loved and supported, which provided avenues to help him change.

While he was on probation, Chris was mandated to do 10 hours of community service a week. The opportunity presented itself to get involved in a county food assistance program. The director of the program made it an easy transition. She seemed very accepting of Chris being involved, even though he was a criminal. Chris did their distribution two days a month and then was eventually permitted to do their homebound program after a year of doing distribution. He worked with homebound people for another seven years and developed personal relationships with many of the clients. Those relationships were really an integral part of his recovery because he felt responsible for these individuals. Eventually, the relationships turned into lasting friendships that are still present today.

The coordinator of the food distribution program gave Chris a bulletin from her church, which highlighted a new program called Celebrate Recovery. Celebrate Recovery is a 12-step program modeled after AA. It opened the door to a whole new community of friends, who are still Chris's friends today. The Celebrate Recovery program actually gave him a different perspective on what it is to be a man. They provided books to read because Chris's real problem was that he did not respect or stand up for himself in healthy ways. Chris came to believe that an interesting aspect of addiction is that emotional maturity stops when individuals start to use substances. He also thought that if individuals use substances to deal with reality, their maturity gets stunted or pushed down and they are not able to identify their feelings.

Through Celebrate Recovery, Chris had a new community and was learning new ways of changing himself. For example, Chris was involved in a relationship that was not very healthy. Although the relationship ended, it taught him that he did not know how to ask for what he needed. He did not know how to stand up for himself and say no. So the next year he was really learning about how to be assertive and to get his needs met. In time, the Celebrate

Recovery program would help him become more assertive in relationships and his life.

Chris was influenced by others in his life during the recovery process. He met another man who would serve as a mentor. According to Chris, this man was the first person he ever met who knew who he was and what his limitations were. This mentor was very wise, wealthy, and had everything you could imagine. He traveled a lot and sent Chris postcards. Just that act of sending Chris a postcard was love. This man really cared about Chris and was not afraid to show it. Chris would later say that he learned more from this mentor than any other person in his life.

Chris also became involved with other community programs, such as the County Alliance Against Drugs, the County Meth Task Force, and the Guidance Center; the latter was a program involved in kids' lives and drugs. Chris also worked in the adult residential unit for four years. He really wanted to be involved with the meth task force because he thought sometimes politicians and nonaddicted individuals lacked insight about addiction. Being an addict in recovery, he wanted to have a voice for other addicts. His community had expanded, and he saw aspects of the recovery process he would not be aware of if he had not been participating. He met great people; intelligent people who helped him grow.

During his recovery process, Chris started attending community college. Chris believed college was going to help him grow up and develop educational self-esteem. He did fairly well in college the first semester and got an A. He took a full course load the next semester and seven years thereafter. He had doubts at times but had a strong sense of purpose. He had to ask for help and had needed a math tutor twice. Years ago he would never have asked for a tutor because he was too proud. All of these people came into Chris's life at the right time. Eventually, he earned an associate's degree in psychology and a master's degree in social work. College helped him realize he was capable of making it. College, community service, and the 12-step program also helped him with his social self-esteem. He always felt comfortable with older people, but talking with peers was always difficult and created anxiety for him. He concluded that his alcohol use in the beginning relieved his anxiety a bit, but the problem was that he became an addict.

CHRIS'S LIFE TODAY

Chris's life in recovery was completely different. He had hope, not just hope that he could keep himself from getting into trouble again. He hoped that he could live a sober life and then become the kind of person who could sustain it. He knew that he also needed to continue the change process, so he focused tremendous energy on his recovery. It became his passion and his highest priority. It has now been almost eight years since his arrest, and Chris has continued to serve his community and to help other people in recovery.

Today, Chris attributes much of his recovery to the community that embraced him. Being immersed in the home of his friend directly out of jail, who offered him unconditional love and support, gave him hope. Chris, seeing the other students in the home being successful, was inspired. He craved what they had. His mentor made the process of his going back to school possible. The encouragement from others was essential to his recovery.

Working with the food distribution program gave him the opportunity to become involved in the community. For Chris to develop organizational skills was important. The director of the program gave Chris needed support for him to go to college. She lessened his fears and told him what to expect. For Chris, having her support was critical.

Today, Chris lives a very structured life. He writes down what he needs to be and do each day and every hour of the day. He has accountability to his sponsor, who helps him to grow spiritually and gain wisdom. Chris has accountability partners who encourage him. He has a job that provides avenues of service to others and challenges him to continue to grow as a person. He stays open to ideas and looks for others to mentor him through life. In turn, he mentors three young men, which provides him with opportunities to practice patience, kindness, tolerance, and most important, love. He finds it incredible to be involved with their lives and watch them grow as men. He gets to direct his passions in areas that he feels are essential for addicts and the community to grow. He continues to meet people who are as passionate as him to see this redemptive community come to light. He absolutely wants the best for his community, and this means everyone. He feels relationships and community are at the core of successful recovery.

TWO STORIES AND TWO DIFFERENT OUTCOMES

The stories of Sasha and Chris illustrate the important role the community can play in recovery from meth addiction. Sasha and Chris were both introduced to meth through friends and close associates. These so-called friends supported their meth involvement, even when they knew it would be detrimental to Sasha and Chris—the proverbial misery that loves company. It is clear that Sasha was used by her boyfriend and others in the immediate meth-using group. Sasha and Chris were able to conceal their use from loved ones over extended spans of time, often relying on lies and deceit to manipulate others and continue their use. Both tried to stop, Sasha multiple times, only to fall back into the grasp of the drug.

Sasha was tragically unsuccessful in separating herself from her involvement with the meth group. The meth-using group, especially her best friend, kept drawing her back into negativity and self-harming behavior. Her well-intentioned, loving parents tried to do what was best for her through traditional services, sometimes relying on them and other times trying to avoid them. They became desperate, which only made matters worse. In their hearts and minds, they wanted so much to believe her and consequently fell victim to her manipulations.

Ultimately, what led to Sasha's spiral down and tragic death was not only her heavy involvement with meth but also the failure of the community to provide her with what she needed, support and love. The community did not hold her accountable for her actions, provide her with needed structure, and address her poor eating habits and corresponding poor health. In addition, the community failed to help her get away from her meth-using friends. She was left to go it alone, and that was too much for her to handle.

In contrast, Chris was able to overcome his involvement with meth. The key difference was the role community played in his life. Chris was eventually able to overcome his involvement with meth and enter into sobriety, but only with the help of those around him. For Chris, a combination of events, outside support, influential individuals, structure, beliefs, accountability, spirituality, hope, faith, and some personal decisions led to his sobriety. Chris also addressed his eating and health issues. He learned that others cared for and supported him and that there was another way to live.

CHAPTER 3

What Is Meth?

The stories of Sasha and Chris illustrate some very important aspects of addiction to methamphetamine that make it truly a unique drug. Their stories also help shed light on the culture of people who use meth and the distinct, powerful dynamics that are characteristic of these groups of people. Most important, however, is how the stories of Sasha and Chris help to demonstrate what families and communities can do to help those who become addicted to meth. That difficult issue is really the main topic of this book, and the stories of Sasha and Chris help to show what families and communities can do to help the process of meth recovery. Their stories also show that there are things that families and communities can do that may seem beneficial, but which are actually counterproductive to the treatment process. Before discussing how families and communities can intervene to help treat meth addiction, it is important to first go into more detail about the drug itself and its uniqueness. An informed community-based approach to treating meth addiction is critical, so that efforts can target the unique aspects of meth that might be missed otherwise.

To many people, understanding meth can be confusing. Once a person has started using heavily and they have become involved with others who are using, their life can become chaotic and unpredictable. There is very little about their behavior that makes sense. This could plainly be seen in the stories of Sasha and Chris. Because of their addiction to meth, they seemed set on pursuing a path of destruction that others around them could not understand. Fortunately for Chris and those close to him, that pattern was broken, and he is now living a sober and happy life. Unfortunately and tragically for Sasha and for those who love her, that pattern was not broken.

There are many unique effects and issues associated with meth use. For this reason, it is helpful to sort them into distinct categories of understanding. The three categories of the unique effects and issues associated with meth used in this book are the biological, psychological, and social domains. It is important to point out that while it is helpful to untangle how meth has affected someone's life into these three domains, doing so is really an artificial simplification of how the addicted persons, their family, and their community may experience their addiction to meth. In other words, the addicted individuals do not clearly differentiate their involvement in meth into these three categories. For them, it occurs all together with effects and issues from all three domains influencing one another (see figure 3.1). All these create extreme disruption in the user's lifestyle and significant deterioration in the person's level of overall functioning. Artificial as it may be, sorting the effects and issues of meth abuse into these domains provides a starting point for understanding meth, what it does to people who use it, and most important, how to help them.

Figure 3.1
The Domains of Methamphetamine Addiction

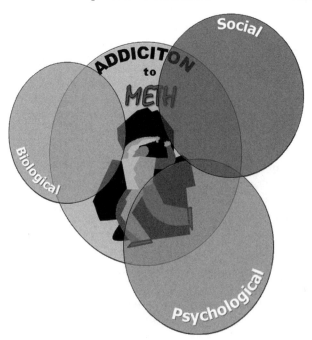

Source: Dr. Nicolas Taylor, 2008.

BIOLOGICAL EFFECTS OF METHAMPHETAMINE

Similar to cocaine, meth is a stimulant drug, but how it affects the brain is quite distinct. To appreciate how meth affects brain and then how these effects in turn influence behavior, thoughts, and moods, it is important to first have an understanding of how the brain works. The functioning of the human brain is really the most impressive technology on the planet. There is nothing that compares to the human brain in terms of its complexity and sophistication.

The computer, while a good model for understanding the activity of the brain, has not come close to replicating it. All human experience is tied to this one distinct organ. Activity in the brain intricately affects all of our human experiences, such as thought, emotion, memory, intention, desire, hope, and action. To see how activity in the brain influences every aspect of our human experience and how the effect of a drug like meth on the brain can alter our experience so significantly, it is important to understand how the brain itself works.

Looking at the whole brain as an organ tells us very little about the complexity of what the brain does, no more than looking at the outer shell of a computer tells us much about what that particular computer might be capable of doing. It is more about the components of the computer and about the interaction of these components that help to account for a computer's function and capacity. Perhaps, an even better computer model for understanding cerebral functioning is that of the Internet. The emergence of the Internet has entirely changed personal computing. Prior to the Internet, information searches were limited to what was stored on local computer memory sources, including floppy discs, hard drives, and/or CD-ROMs. After the appearance of the Internet, suddenly the opportunity to exchange and process information increased exponentially by the number of computers and servers added to the Web.

The functioning of the human brain is comparable. The activity of the brain is more about how individual brain cells communicate with one another, organize, and synchronize processes of these communications than about the organ as a whole. Brain cells, called neurons, communicate with one another via the release of chemical messengers called neurotransmitters. Within an individual neuron, a message originates as a collective electrical charge, which, when it reaches a certain threshold, triggers the transmission of an electrical and mechanical signal down a neural pathway known as the neuron's axon. The message traveling down the axon is known as an action potential. The end of the axon is the terminal button. At this spot, the axon junctions with other neurons, muscles, glands, or organs. In the terminal button, the electrical and chemical message of the action potential is transduced, or changed, into a chemical message. This occurs as the signal of the action potential triggers storage sacs (called vesicles) for neurotransmitter chemical messengers to travel to the inner wall of the terminal button and then to release out of the neuron the neurotransmitters into an area between the terminal button and the signal-receiving neuron, gland, muscle, or organ. This small space is called the synaptic gap. The signal-sending neuron is called the presynaptic neuron and the signal-receiving neuron is called the postsynaptic neuron. The neurotransmitters released into the synaptic gap travel across the gap and then chemically "plug" into special proteins on the postsynaptic neuron called neuroreceptors.

Neurotransmitters match with specific neuroreceptors like a key in a lock; they activate the receptor and change the electrical charge in the receiving neuron. Therefore, once the neurotransmitters plug into the neuroreceptors, the message of the presynaptic neuron is transmitted to the postsynaptic neuron as the neurotransmitters trigger a change in the electrical charge of the signal-receiving neuron (see figure 3.2).

Different neurotransmitters have different effects on signal-receiving neurons. Some neurotransmitters have an excitatory effect, meaning that they increase the cumulative charge inside the neuron, thus increasing the likelihood that the charge within the neuron will pass the threshold and create the all-or-nothing firing of the action potential. Other neurotransmitters are inhibitory; they act to decrease the cumulative charge inside the signal-receiving neuron after they have plugged into their specific neuroreceptors. This action decreases the likelihood that the neuron will fire.

The neurotransmitters that are primarily affected by the action of methamphetamine include a group classified as the catecholamines (dopamine, norepinephrine, and epinephrine) and serotonin. All of these neurotransmitters are excitatory, meaning that as a drug like meth increases their release, they increase the activities of the neurons they affect. Dopamine is the primary neurotransmitter responsible for the sense of euphoric pleasure meth users experience, although increases in serotonin elevate mood as well. The effect of specific neurotransmitters can vary depending on where on the brain the activity of the neurotransmitter is affected. For example, while increased release of dopamine induces feelings of pleasure, it can also interfere with voluntary motor responses, making the user somewhat restless and jittery. Serotonin elevates mood, but it also can create psychotic processing, such as hallucinations and delusions. The effect of meth on epinephrine and norepinephrine release is what accounts primarily for the increased energy,

Figure 3.2
Neural Communication

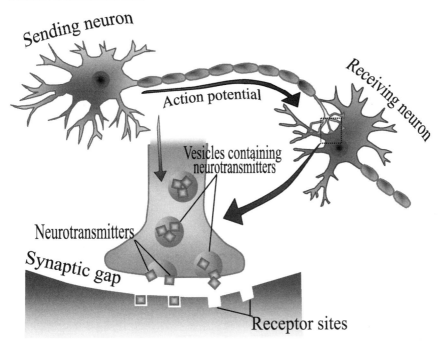

Source: Drawing by Dr. Nicolas Taylor, 2008.

hyperkinetic behaviors, and general stimulating properties associated with meth use. The increases in norepinephrine account mostly for sleeplessness.

The process of neurotransmitter release is managed by two systems of excess neurotransmitter deactivation and one system of release regulation. Leftover neurotransmitters that do not plug into neuroreceptor sites are taken back into the presynaptic neuron through a mechanism known as reuptake. Excess neurotransmitters are also deactivated and cleared from the synaptic gap through degrading enzymes that break them down. The threshold release level for neurotransmitters is determined, in part, by the activity of similar neuroreceptors on the presynaptic neuron called autoreceptors. When neurotransmitter release reaches the point at which the autoreceptors are activated, this signals the presynaptic neuron to discontinue release.

To understand exactly how meth affects neurotransmitter activity, it is helpful to contrast the pharmacokinetic properties of meth with those of its

Figure 3.3
The Effects of Cocaine on Neural Communication

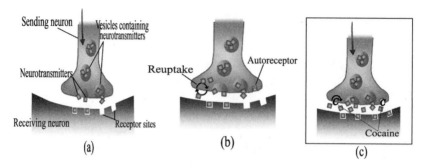

Neurotransmitters carry a message from a sending neuron across a synapse to receptor sites on a receiving neuron.	The sending neuron normally reabsorbs excess neurotransmitter molecules through a process called reuptake and autoreceptors on the sending neuron regulate neurotransmitter release.	By binding to the sites that normally reabsorb neurotransmitter molecules, cocaine blocks reuptake of dopamine, norepinephrine, and serotonin. Cocaine also blocks the autoreceptor. These actions lead to unregulated release of neurotransmitters with no reuptake. Extra neurotransmitters remain in the synapse intensifying their normal mood-altering effects and producing a euphoric rush. When the cocaine level drops, depleted supplies of these neurotransmitters produce a crash.

Source: Dr. Nicolas Taylor, 2008.

sister stimulant drug, cocaine (see figure 3.3). Cocaine impacts the release of the neurotransmitters dopamine, serotonin, and epinephrine. The pleasure-producing effects of cocaine are accounted for by the action of cocaine on dopamine and serotonin, while the stimulating properties of cocaine are mainly because of its effect on epinephrine. Cocaine blocks the reuptake of these three neurotransmitters and thus increases their activity by limiting their deactivation. In addition, cocaine blocks the autoreceptors for these neurotransmitters by inhibiting the shutoff for their release. As a result, the presynaptic neuron is exhausted of its neurotransmitter supplies as it continues release. The inhibition of reuptake means that the neurotransmitter activity on receptor sites on the postsynaptic neuron continues excessively, producing a heightened effect.

The action of meth on the process of neuronal communication is quite distinct compared to that of cocaine, although they are both stimulant drugs. In addition to dopamine, serotonin, and epinephrine, meth also affects the activity of the neurotransmitter norepinephrine, which partially accounts for the extended stimulating effects of meth. The effects of cocaine can last as long as 60 to 120 minutes, depending on the user's level of tolerance, purity of the drug, and route of administration. In comparison, the effects of equal doses of meth can endure 16 to 20 hours, usually 8 to 10 times the duration of equal doses of cocaine.

The specific pharmacologic effect of meth is different from cocaine as well. Meth penetrates into the presynaptic neuron and causes vesicle sacs to leak neurotransmitters in the cytoplasm of the cell. Meth also affects the outer membrane of the presynaptic neuron, causing the neurotransmitters to leak uncontrollably into the synaptic gap. The excessive release of neurotransmitters from the vesicles, and then out of the neuron itself, increases neurotransmitter activity in the synaptic gap (see figure 3.4). This completely overwhelms the processes of reuptake and enzymatic breakdown.

One very unique characteristic of meth is that it is neurotoxic, meaning that its action on brain cells may cause irreversible cell damage. The neurotoxic effects of meth occur because as neurotransmitters are leaked into the cytoplasm of the presynaptic neuron, the neurotransmitters are broken down by enzymes. This breakdown process is usually harmless, but when excessive, such as that caused by meth, toxic and reactive chemicals are produced

Figure 3.4
The Effects of Meth on the Neuron

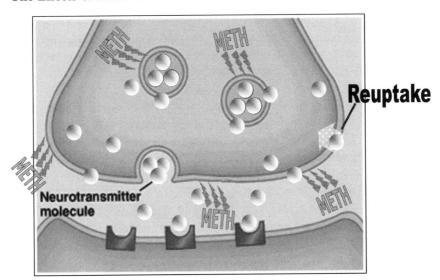

Source: Drawing by Dr. Nicolas Taylor, 2008.

essentially poisoning the neuron. The longer duration of meth means that these neurotoxic effects endure over longer periods of time and the affected neurons atrophy and eventually die.

Neuroimages of brain activity, such as photon emission tomography and single photon emission computerized tomography scans, as well as images of brain structure, such as magnetic resonance imaging, have shown clear signs of decreased functionality. In some cases, even loss of brain tissue was related to extended meth use. The exact deficits produced by the neurotoxicity of meth depend, of course, on the length of use and the amount used, the exact part of the brain most affected, and the neuroresilience of the user.

Biological effects of meth use can be divided into those associated with intoxication and those associated with toxicity. Of course, effects associated with intoxication are expected to subside with the termination of use, while the effects due to toxicity are expected to endure and be long term. Meth intoxication produces elevated body temperature, blood pressure, heart rate, and muscle tension. People under the influence of meth have also been found to be hyperdistractible, to have poor impulse control, tactile sensations, personality changes, and short-term memory deficits. These are all related to the specific effects of meth on several parts of the brain.

Studies have shown clear detrimental impacts of extended meth use that persist post-use, which seem to be related to neurotoxicity. These effects include memory impairment, paranoia, anhedonia (diminished ability to feel pleasure), and attention-related difficulties. Some of the effects of meth can be accounted for by its impact on the activity of dopamine in several parts of the brain, including the striatum (which is made up of caudate and putamen) and the prefrontal cortex. Other effects of meth are related to its impact on serotonin activity in, among other areas, the parietal cortex and the hippocampus.

Within the striatum is an interesting junction of dopaminergic neurons known as the nucleus accumbens. The nucleus accumbens has attracted the attention of researchers for decades since its discovery by James Olds in the 1950s. The nucleus accumbens is an important link in the brain's pleasure pathway. Animals trained to self-stimulate by pressing a lever that activates an electrode planted on the nucleus accumbens will choose pressing the lever to the exclusion of other activities, including eating, sleeping, and caring for the young (see figure 3.5). When required to cross an electrified grid, which delivers a very painful electric shock in order to get to the lever, animals will endure more pain than even starving animals would endure to get to food. The experience of the nucleus accumbens' being stimulated has been likened to the feeling of pleasure experienced during a sexual orgasm. While most

Figure 3.5
Rat Self-Stimulating the Nucleus Accumbens

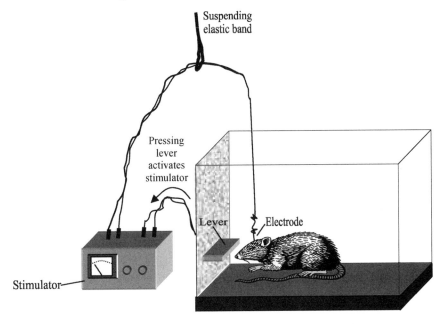

Source: Drawing by Dr. Nicolas Taylor, 2008.

substances of abuse seem to stimulate the nucleus accumbens to some degree, stimulant drugs like cocaine and meth seem to have the most pronounced effect on this natural reward system.

Meth also appears to affect the activity of dopamine in the prefrontal cortex. The frontal lobe of the cerebral cortex is important in complex executive functioning behaviors, such as planning, managing emotion, and placing controls on behavior. The effect of meth on the serotonergic neurons of the parietal lobe helps account for telltale fine motor behaviors associated with excessive meth use, such as fidgeting and, even more particularly, picking of the skin. Within the parietal lobe are bands of sensory and motor cortices. These parts of the brain are interesting because their surface areas appear to be topographic in that stimulating particular regions produces both sensations of being touched in certain skin areas and motor responses from certain body parts. Erratic firing of the sensory and motor neurons within the parietal lobe may account for the tactical hallucinations associated with meth use and with the subsequent picking behaviors that produce skin lesions and sores. Also impacted by meth is serotonergic activity within the hippocampus region of both the right and the left temporal lobes. The hippocampus regions are essential in memory function; disruption of processing in the hippocampus can affect both short- and long-term memory.

PSYCHOLOGICAL EXPLANATIONS

Psychological theories of human behavior can be helpful in understanding addiction to meth. The behavioral theory of operant conditioning posits that behaviors that produce desirable outcomes will be repeated, while those that produce undesirable outcomes will be abandoned. Outcomes, or consequences of behavior, which have the effect of increasing the likelihood that a behavior will occur again in the future are referred to as reinforcing, while consequences of behavior which decrease the likelihood that a behavior will be repeated are referred to as being punishing. Outcomes that reinforce behavior can do so either because they involve "turning on" something pleasant or desirable (such as receiving money, praise, attention, food, or prizes) or because they "turn off" things that are noxious, unpleasant, or undesirable (such as pain, discomfort, stress, fatigue, or cravings). Consequences of behavior that "turn on" desirable outcomes are referred to as positive reinforcement, and consequences that "turn off" undesirable, unpleasant, or painful experiences are referred to as negative reinforcement (see table 3.1).

Meth is so powerfully addicting because it produces both positive and negative reinforcement. Immediately following ingestion, users of meth feel a rush of pleasure, a sense of euphoria, a sense of false competency, power, control, and a heightened level of self-esteem. Just as important, or perhaps even more important, is the fact that immediately following ingestion, users of meth experience relief from feelings of cravings, fatigue, depression, self-loathing, and/or low self-esteem.

At this point, it is important to note just how powerful negative reinforcement or the taking away of unpleasant, undesirable, or painful feelings really is. Human beings certainly are pleasure seeking; however, they are also pain

Table 3.1
Operant Conditioning

	Turns on	Turns off
Pleasant	Positive reinforcement	Negative punishment
Unpleasant	Positive punishment	Negative reinforcement

Source: Dr. Nicolas Taylor, 2008.

avoiding, and if given the choice to feel pleasure or avoid pain, they will often choose the latter. This can be clearly observed in the example of an individual whose most desirable food is a tasty dessert, such as banana cream pie. If this person is feeling nauseated and is given the choice to either eat a slice of banana cream pie or take an antinausea pill, the person will choose to take the pill because relief of the feelings of nausea is more important even than the pleasurable taste of the banana cream pie.

The power of negative reinforcement helps explain why meth can become so addicting. Initially, someone may start using the drug because of the pleasant feelings it turns on. However, with progression there is also usually an increase of undesirable or unpleasant outcomes associated with chronic meth use such as legal problems, alienation from family, loss of job, health problems, changes in appearance, and so forth. With these unwanted or undesirable outcomes come feelings of despair, frustration, depression, and low self-esteem. The use of meth then becomes more enticing not only because of the positive feelings it creates but also, perhaps even more significant, because of what it takes away. Therefore, the fact that meth is both a positive and a negative reinforcer helps to explain not only initial use but also progression leading to chronic addiction.

An interesting correlation exists between the desirable and the undesirable effects of meth. The desirable effects, such as the positive and negative reinforcement just described, tend to occur quickly, almost immediately after use. Therefore, they are referred to as proximal effects. However, with the passage of time and ongoing use, a clear diminishing of these desirable effects is experienced by the chronic user, in an almost diametric fashion. There is a converse increase of the undesirable effects of the drug, which include symptoms of paranoia, mistrust, agitation, violent behavior, psychosis, and cognitive decompensation (see figure 3.6). Because these effects occur further down the line following initial use, they are referred to as distal effects. Other effects, which are not directly related to the consumption of the drug but instead to the effect it has on a user's lifestyle, can include things like legal problems, loss of freedom, jail time, and alienation from family, loss of prized possessions and objects, low self-esteem, and self-disgust. As was mentioned earlier, with increasing patterns of use, there does tend to be an increase in the experience of these unpleasant outcomes.

Returning then to the model of operant conditioning, the turning on of desirable experiences and the turning off of pain or unpleasant experiences are reinforcing in that they make it more likely for the behavior to occur again. Some behaviors are punishing in that they either "turn on" unpleasant or undesirable outcomes or they "turn off" things that are pleasurable or

Figure 3.6
The Effects of Meth Over Time

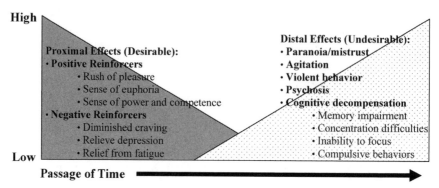

Source: Dr. Nicolas Taylor, 2008.

desirable. Consequences of behavior that "turn on" unpleasant or unwanted outcomes are referred to as positive punishment, while consequences of behavior that "turn off" pleasant or desirable things are referred to as negative punishment. Both of these kinds of outcomes tend to have the effect of diminishing the likelihood that a behavior might occur again. In the case of meth addiction, meth clearly produces both positive and negative punishment, causing an increase of unpleasant outcomes. Situations such as having to face a punitive judge, an increase in disappointment, frustration and anger from loved ones, and even the physical discomfort associated with the unhealthy lifestyle are all examples of positive punishment. Negative punishment occurs because the use of meth creates situations in which the meth user is losing things that are important to him or her such as freedom, important relationships, money, self-esteem, employment opportunities, time with family, and even custody of children (see table 3.2).

Given meth produces notably powerful positive and negative punishments, it would be expected that most users, upon experiencing these unpleasant outcomes, would discontinue using the drug. This obviously is not the case in the lives of many chronic users. There are several reasons why punishment or unpleasant outcomes simply do not work to deter the addicted individual from using meth.

The first reason has to do with timing. As was mentioned previously, the punishing effects of meth use occur later in a using episode, whereas the reinforcing effects of meth use occur immediately after use. This difference in timing is significant since the user is often looking to feel pleasure and turn off pain immediately, regardless of what may happen down the line.

Table 3.2
Operant Conditioning Applied to Meth

	Turns on	Turns off
Pleasant	Feelings of euphoria	Freedom
	Sense of competency	Closeness with family
	Orgasmic pleasure	Self-respect
	Heightened self-esteem	Lifestyle stability
Unpleasant	Jail	Depression
	Legal problems	Low self-esteem
	Poor health	Self-disgust
	Self-loathing	Feelings of shame

Source: Dr. Nicolas Taylor, 2008.

Complicating matters even further is the fact that some of these undesirable effects do not occur every time the addicted individual uses meth. For example, an addicted individual does not get thrown in jail every time he or she uses meth, nor does the individual have to go in front of a punitive judge or disappointed parent or loved one every time the person uses it. Often, people around addicted individuals are not fully aware of their use. Therefore, they are able to continue using it with little or no negative consequences.

Another reason why punishing outcomes does not always deter an addict has to do with the power of negative reinforcement that was mentioned earlier. Even though negative consequences may come because of an addict's use, the relief from pain and unpleasant feelings is often so important and so powerful that it drives behavior, especially because that relief is provided immediately following use.

Models of classical conditioning are also helpful in understanding meth use. Classical conditioning, also referred to as Pavlovian or respondent conditioning, is a psychological theory used to explain why human beings develop almost reflex-like associations between certain neutral cues and other meaningful cues with which they are paired. For example, classical conditioning can be used to explain why it is that someone who has been in a winter driving accident begins to feel anxious whenever he or she has to drive in the snow. Before the conditioning event, the accident in this case, the individual likely felt little or at least less anxiety about driving in the snow. After the accident, however, the person has developed an almost reflex-like association between snow and the accident such that even the thought of snow itself may cause feelings of anxiety. This may happen, not because snow is particularly harmful or fear provoking, but because of the learned association between snow and the accident. Before the conditioning event, snow would be labeled a neutral stimulus. The accident itself would be labeled an unconditioned stimulus, and the anxiety associated with being in the accident, an unconditioned response because the anxiety from the accident is natural and happens almost like an automatic response. After conditioning, however, the neutral stimulus of snow takes on the meaning of the accident itself. Even though the snow itself does not cause an accident to happen, the individual experiences anxiety even just thinking about snow. Snow becomes a conditioned stimulus, and anxiety produced just by thinking about snow or driving in snow is the conditioned response.

Classical conditioning can also explain why it is that people may hate or love certain smells. Perfume and cologne are good examples of this. If a person is with someone who always wears a certain perfume or cologne and if that person happens to really like him or her, then the smell alone of the perfume or cologne will trigger the pleasant feelings of like, and even love or infatuation. If, on the other hand, a couple, for example, is forced to be with someone they really do not like for whatever reasons and that person always wears a certain perfume or cologne, then they are likely to have bad feelings whenever they smell that particular perfume or cologne in the future. Classical conditioning, of course, has to do with memory. The learned associations are so automatic that they often occur even before the person had had time to consciously think of the memory. The learned associations become almost like a reflex. That is why classical conditioning has also been referred to as reflexive conditioning.

Before discussing classical conditioning and its application to meth addiction, it is first helpful to compare the quality of conditioned responses with the quality of unconditioned responses. Conditioned responses are those responses that occur because of a conditioning event. They are triggered because a previously neutral stimulus, such as snow, has been paired with an unconditioned stimulus, such as an accident. The now conditioned stimulus of snow may cause feelings of anxiety, which is the conditioned response. The unconditioned response is always the natural reflex that is automatically triggered by the unconditioned stimulus. In the case of the person who was in the winter driving accident, the unconditioned stimulus is the accident, and the unconditioned response is the very natural reflex-like response of anxiety. In the case of pleasurable feelings that come from the perfume commonly worn by a loved one, the unconditioned stimulus is the loved one and the unconditioned response is the pleasurable feeling triggered by this person. The smell of perfume is the conditioned stimulus, and the good feelings the person has smelling it is the conditioned response. Conditioned and unconditioned responses are actually the same response. The difference between responses is that one is triggered by a stimulus, while the other is a learned association. Conditioned responses are triggered not because of a natural reflex but because of an association with another meaningful stimulus. What is important to remember, especially as applied to meth use, is that the conditioned stimulus is always qualitatively less than the unconditioned stimulus. In other words, the response that comes because of a learned association is always less than the response that occurs as a reflex. Anxiety caused by thinking about snow or even that caused by having to drive in snow is always less than anxiety caused by the accident itself. The pleasure that is felt just smelling someone's perfume is less than the pleasure that is felt by being around that person.

The model of classical conditioning applied to meth use actually applies to the use of almost all substances of abuse, just more so with meth. Applying classical conditioning to meth use begins with an analysis of the unconditioned stimuli of naturally pleasurable activities or events, such as a celebration or having fun with friends. Most people feel pleasure in response to these things, and those feelings of pleasure happen naturally. We did not have to be taught to feel good in response to naturally pleasurable things. For some people, these naturally pleasurable events can be relaxing and talking with friends after a long day or week of work. For others, it may be enjoying an activity such as fishing, hiking, or rafting. What tends to happen is that many people will enliven their pleasurable activities with the use of drugs or alcohol. There is a pairing that occurs between the pleasurable activities and the use of an addictive substance. Friends, who might enjoy sitting around on a back patio just talking, drink together as a way of enjoying themselves more. Watching a sporting event is enlivened by drinking as well. For some people, the pairing of naturally pleasurable events with the use of drugs and alcohol can become so automatic that in time the pleasurable event actually becomes all about the use of chemicals. A wedding, which for some people is enjoyable because it is a celebration of the new union of two people and a time for friends and family to get together, can be for other people seen as an occasion to drink and/or use drugs to excess. Going to a party, for some, has less to do with the other people attending and the activities they will organize than it is about the substances they will abuse while at the party. Pleasure, which may have been experienced because of the naturally pleasurable event, becomes lost because of their use of drugs and/or alcohol. The pleasurable experience, whatever it may have been, becomes more about the substance high than it is about whatever good feelings that may have come from the experience itself.

Theoretically, classical conditioning helps us to understand why this occurs. Naturally pleasurable experiences such as spending time with loved ones, enjoying a hobby, or celebrating something exciting are all unconditioned stimuli. The pleasure that comes from doing these things is the unconditioned response, which occurs almost as a reflex. For example, most people do not have to be taught to feel good when they hold a small infant or play with a puppy. The associated good feelings happen naturally. The feelings are unconditioned responses to the unconditioned stimuli of enjoyable events. However, when drugs or alcohol, and meth especially, are repeatedly combined with the pleasurable activities, then these substances become conditioned stimuli, and the pleasure that is experienced becomes conditioned responses triggered by the substance use. Most important is the fact that just as the pleasure that comes from smelling a loved one's perfume is less than the pleasure associated with being with that loved one, the pleasure that comes from using drugs, even powerful drugs like meth, is less than the pleasure derived from the naturally pleasurable event.

This may not seem true at first glance, as people talk about the immense rush of pleasure they experience when they use a drug like meth or when people who use meth are observed giving up things that are important to them simply for the rush of doing the drug. Surely, the pleasure from meth must be greater than the pleasure that comes from naturally pleasurable activities, such as playing with one's children or engaging in a favorite hobby. Otherwise, people would do those things instead of using the drug. This is true, but only if we consider the feelings of pleasure that are immediately derived from the use of meth. As was mentioned earlier, with ongoing use those feelings begin to dissipate, and then the user is often left with even stronger feelings of despair and cravings to use the drug again. This leads to ongoing meth use as a form of negative reinforcement. So the pleasure that comes from using meth, even if it lasts for a couple of days during a binge use, is still fleeting and false, whereas the pleasure that comes from naturally pleasurable activities is much more enduring. Even more important, naturally pleasurable activities are much more satisfying in the end.

It is important for people addicted to meth to understand this comparison. It is hard to do, and many people who use meth do so because they never learned how to associate feelings of pleasure with naturally pleasurable events in the first place. Either it was modeled for them by other substance-abusing family members at an early age that to feel good you had to use a substance perhaps, or they may have also started abusing substances at such an early age that they never learned to experience pleasure naturally. For as long as they can remember, they used drugs or alcohol as a way of feeling good.

As can be recalled from the discussion of operant conditioning, meth use is reinforcing both because of the positive feelings it turns on and because of the unpleasant feelings it turns off. The association between substance abuse and feeling good is not just tied to deriving feelings of pleasure but also to strategies to avoid pain. In other words, the young person who from an early age witnessed others using substances as a way of having a good time probably also witnessed people using substances as a way of removing or managing painful feelings.

Chronic users associate their meth use to feeling good, and not bad, to the point that it is a reflexive response in their lives. If users have grown up without coping skills, short of their drug use, they struggle with issues in their lives. They also lack the abilities to enjoy doing things without drugs and to help themselves through difficult challenges. It is as if they were developmentally halted. When they should have been learning and acquiring the skills of feeling good about themselves, and coping skills, without the use of any mood-altering chemical, they were high. Not uncommonly, people who have used meth and then stop later in their lives complain that they feel as if they are young people trapped in adult bodies. They have developmental delays in their coping skills.

SOCIAL ISSUES UNIQUE TO METH

People familiar with meth are aware of the unique subculture of people who tend to use together. The sordid, and undesirable, subculture of meth use is insidious, and it tends to be self-protective and self-consuming. While members of the meth subculture will commonly steal from one another, sleep with one another's romantic partners, and even sexually abuse one another's children or teenage daughters, when one is in trouble and is being sought by the authorities or sober community, there is a protective fellowship that develops and meth addicts help each other out of trouble.

Often the groups of people who use meth together are as addicting as the drug itself. That may seem odd to people who have never used meth because the groups of people using meth are not that enticing, based on many other standards. While there may be quite a bit of trafficking that does take place with meth and the manufacturing of meth may present an opportunity to sell a lot of the drug for very little cost, there is certainly not a sense of glamour or prestige associated with being someone involved with others who use meth. A very convincing use prevention commercial called "junkie den," produced by the Montana Meth Project, depicts a young man using meth with other people obviously older than him by at least several years. After his first use, the lead junkie informs him that he was now one of them and that all they were experiencing was now his. The commercial then shows the filth and squalor of the meth-using group. The young man counters the statement of the junkie and insists that he did not want what they have and that he intended to use meth just one time, at which all of the junkies begin laughing. The point of the commercial that with even just one use people, especially young people, can be hooked for life and unavoidably tied in with the meth-using community is debatable. However, there are powerful social forces at play, creating a dynamic of group inclusion and seclusion. Once a person has started using meth and is involved with others who do it as well, it becomes very difficult to stop.

Meth-using groups have their own norms and standards governing the behaviors of the group. In most meth groups, there are really only two admission requirements. First, of course, is that you have to use meth with them. Second is simply that you keep what the group does and who belongs to it secret from nonusers. In other words, you help protect the group from outside forces, individuals, or agencies such as law enforcement, child protection case workers, and confidential informants, who might threaten the group. There is nothing worse than getting caught, and there is no one worse than someone who turns you in. Snitches are placed at the bottom of every social order in the meth-using world. It is more acceptable to steal from family members, abuse and neglect dependent children, beat women, commit fraud and theft that victimizes senior citizens than it is to snitch out on other people who use meth. Snitching is the worst crime that can be committed, and in some circles, it is considered worthy of capital punishment. It has been said in more than one meth-using community, "The only good snitch is a dead snitch."

This is driven by the fact that those who are in the meth-using community are guilty of having committed a number of legal offences and only a few have never stayed completely out of legal entanglements. More commonly, incidents of domestic violence, driving under the influence, theft, identity fraud, and check fraud have led most people who abuse meth to have encountered legal systems at least once in their lives. Those who abuse meth and who may have never faced legal charges are rare, and rarer are those who have never had dealings with child welfare systems. More commonly, child protection services have become aware of the meth-using household in which children live and have intervened typically by removing the children from the home. Child protection then develops a treatment plan with the meth-using parent or parents.

In addition, meth users who already have legal problems fear getting caught largely due to the drug itself. Meth use can lead to paranoia. In cases of chronic use, paranoia can become so pronounced that the user literally becomes psychotic. The heavy user of meth can become almost indistinguishable from other psychotic psychiatric patients who suffer from a number of psychological disorders, including paranoid schizophrenia, paranoid personality disorder, bipolar mood disorder, and delusional disorder, persecutory type. The paranoid user's mistrust is turned toward other members of the meth-using community in fear of their "turning one in."

In addition to unwritten norms about "snitching," meth-using communities also tend to have twisted values about parenting. Meth-using parents are considered competent parents as long as they try to leave their child or children in the care of other people when they know they are going to be strung out for a couple of days. Unfortunately, the care the children are left in often comprises other meth users who themselves just do not happen to be strung out at that time. More commonly, the caretakers tend to be the users' parents, who often become the surrogate parents to the child or children.

There also are unwritten norms around love, loyalty, and friendship in the meth-using community. In romantic relationships, companionate love is expressed by being the one person trusted to inject the other partner safely. Friendships are based on watching out for one another to make sure nothing bad happens when their use renders them unable to be conscious enough about what is going on around them to be able to protect themselves. What is interesting is that no matter what norm or standard is used in the meth community, it is always about the dope.

Close analysis of a meth-using community reveals something quite interesting. There do not seem to be any casual or experimental users. These people, often called "chippers," are not well tolerated in the meth-using community because it is quite difficult for users to determine just how safe these people may be. Therefore, the paranoia from meth use creates its own dynamic, whereby those on the periphery of the meth-using community are quickly integrated into the group. Users are either in or out; there is no in between. Therefore, heavy users will often facilitate involvement of peripheral users in an attempt to establish a greater degree of safety. Free or discounted drugs are usually the best way to do this.

Other powerful social forces also act in the progression from peripheral use to heavy involvement. Of course, the addictive properties of the drug itself pull people deeper into use, but changes in social groups affected by changes in daily life patterns also bring this about. When people start using, they may have a job and other social involvements that give them at least some connection with a sober community. As their use progresses, meth use disrupts sleep, and things change. When someone starts using, they may limit it to weekends only, and while they may be a little tired at the start of the week, they will show up to work and maintain some semblance of a normal lifestyle. However, midweek meth use will often begin because of meth's impact on energy increase and/or weight loss. Then, with midweek use even peripheral users start to change their daily living patterns, primarily because they are awake and wanting to be active when the only other people who are awake and wanting to do stuff are other meth addicts.

The disruption of irregular sleep-and-awake cycles on their daily living habits leads to changes in activities as well. People who use meth midweek find it more and more difficult to show up for work or follow through with other social obligations. As the meth-using individuals distance themselves from work and other sober social environments, a natural drift occurs when they begin spending less time with their non-meth-using community and more and more time with people who use meth. As was mentioned, the paranoia of those who use meth encourages this distancing from the sober community out of self-protection. Quickly, the experimental user becomes deeper and deeper involved with meth and other users who often make, traffic, and sell it as well. Difficult as it may seem, the meth-using community becomes like a family to the new addict. They become swallowed up in the whirlpool of chaos that is the life of meth addicts. No one certainly plans for his or her life to go this way, but it just happens gradually at first but then all of a sudden changes.

No discussion of the unique social factors of meth use is complete without something about women and meth. Meth is truly an "equal opportunity destroyer." This is because with all other drugs of abuse higher percentages of men than women end up with severe addiction problems but with meth the proportions are equal. Whether it is hospital discharges for people addicted to meth, treatment admissions, arrests made of people who were high on meth, or coroner's reports that make reference specifically to meth, men and women are equally represented. With meth, inordinately large numbers of women are becoming addicted, compared to men. Obvious questions are why do women use meth and what in the world do women find so appealing about meth that proportionately more of them are using it compared to men?

There are several reasons why this is the case. First, and perhaps most obviously, is women's attraction to weight loss. But also, do not forget, meth provides seemingly endless energy, and women need energy. Sociological studies have found that compared to 30 years ago, expectations of women regarding shared economic responsibilities for households have increased dramatically.

This is in striking contrast to the only slight increase in the expectations of men regarding shared domestic responsibilities. In other words, more and more, the cultural expectation for women is that they do more with less.

As alluring as meth may be for women because of its weight control properties and energy increase, most women addicted to meth report that they started to use meth and then continued using it because of one main factor, a relationship. Meth is quite unique in the way it becomes a part of the way couples relate to one another. That is partially because of the very typical involvement of meth in the couple's sexual experiences. Meth also can become part of how couples relate to one another since often, especially for women, the only person they may trust to administer meth to them intravenously is their romantic partner. This too can stem from the couple's sexual experiences in that the man may take on the roll of the facilitator of the woman's pleasure, via the administration of meth. Similarly, he may assume the same role when bringing her to orgasm. Often, shared meth use is a manifestation of just pure enmeshment. Enmeshment is the blurring of psychological boundaries that occurs when two people become so close and so intertwined that in what they do and think it becomes difficult to determine where one person leaves off and the other begins. Their shared values, feelings, and goals create an interpersonal dynamic in which they act to protect one another from the blatant reality of what they are doing. Besides, as bad as someone's life may be when they are using meth, if they have a partner using with them, that means that at least they are not alone. There is at least one other person who is just as forlorn and miserable as they are and whose life is just as messed up as theirs.

THE HISTORY OF METH

Although we are hearing more and more about it, meth is not a new drug and has been around for decades. Methamphetamine is closely related to the drug amphetamine. Amphetamine was first synthesized in 1887 in Germany by a scientist named L. Edeleano, who named it phenylisopropylamine. During the 1920s, researchers investigated it as a decongestant and as a medical treatment for depression and other medical ailments. By the 1930s, retailers marketed amphetamine as Benzedrine, an over-the-counter decongestant. Later in the decade, physicians prescribed amphetamine for narcolepsy, ADHD, and depression. During World War II, the military used amphetamines to keep soldiers ready and available for duty. As medical use of amphetamines spread, so did abuse.

In 1919, a Japanese chemist named A. Ogata produced the first methamphetamine. Meth is more powerful and easier to manufacture than amphetamine. During World War II, the Japanese military used meth to improve military performance. It was also sold over the counter in Japan to increase work performance and endurance during the war (Anglin et al. 2000). Following the war, its use, including intravenously, became epidemic in Japan, as supplies were readily available (Wermuth 2000). It has been suggested that Adolph Hitler may have been a heavy user.

After World War II, Dexedrine (dextroamphetamine) and Methedrine (luvoamphetamine) became readily available in the United States. College students, truck drivers, motorcycle gangs, and athletes used the drug to stay awake, improve concentration, and performance. By the mid-1960s, people were using meth in San Francisco and parts of the West coast. By 1970, the drug declined following the 1970 Controlled Substances Act, which restricted the production of injectable meth (Wermuth 2000). However, it had made inroads in the gay community by the late 1970s (Bonné 2001). Meth use popularity spread in California during the late 1980s (Leinwand 2003). Hawaii, California, and Arizona were some of the earliest and continue to be the hardest hit states. In 1996, Congress passed the Methamphetamine Control Act of 1996, which doubled the maximum penalties for possession, and increased the penalty for the possession of equipment used to manufacture meth.

By the 1990s, some young adults found meth to be a popular alternative to cocaine and heroin. White motorcycle gangs controlled production and distribution of meth before the 1990s (Gibson, Leamon, and Flynn 2002). Small home labs and Mexican-based criminal organizations eventually took over production and distribution of meth. Mexican-based criminal organizations established "superlabs" in California and Mexico that were capable of producing large amounts of highly pure meth. In Congressional testimony to the Senate Judiciary Committee, authority Donnie R. Marshall reported that about 85 percent of all methamphetamine used in the United States in 2000 was produced by these superlabs (Marshall 2000). During the 1990s— and to the present—another shift occurred as cooks started to produce meth in small, home-based clandestine labs typically located in rural or suburban communities.

The meth on the streets today is often more powerful than that available in earlier years. Today, meth cooks have refined recipes to the point that some batches have as much as six times the potency of meth cooked in the 1960s (Mills 1999). This meth is not always sold on the street, but rather cooks circulate (give or sell) it among friends and acquaintances.

METH AND OTHER STIMULANTS

Meth is a synthetic psychostimulant that physicians have legally prescribed as a treatment for attention deficit disorder under the brand name Desoxyn. The drug can be made easily in clandestine labs with over-the-counter ingredients. For addicts, it is relatively inexpensive to purchase and has desired effects that last for hours. The desired effects of meth use can last from six to eight hours, followed by a coming-down period when the user becomes agitated and potentially violent.

Drugs, such as meth, labeled as psychostimulants include a diverse range of CNS (central nervous system) stimulants such as amphetamine, cocaine, methylphenidate (Ritalin), methylene dioxy-methamphetamine (MDMA, or ecstasy), caffeine, and nicotine, to name a few. A number of prescription drugs, in addition to Ritalin, such as Dexedrine (dextroamphetamine), Cylert (pemoline), and Adderall (adderall) are psychostimulants as well. Psychoactive stimulants activate the CNS by increasing pulse rate, alertness, blood pressure, restlessness, euphoria, excitement, increased energy, talkativeness, and other changes. Users of psychostimulants experience euphoria, increased sense of well-being, more energy, more confidence or overconfidence, improved cognitive and psychomotor performance, suppression of appetite, and insomnia.

Users of stimulants experience "highs," which are a temporary heightened sense of euphoria during a portion of the stimulant's use. With use, the user runs the risk of not being able to sleep, becoming violent, paranoid, anxious, depressed, and losing interest in food. Major stimulants are amphetamines, cocaine and crack, methylphenidate, and methamphetamine. Other minor stimulants include or are found in caffeine, chocolate, nicotine, and tea. Meth can be compared to other categories of drugs and substances such as alcohol, but most commonly it is compared to the stimulant cocaine.

Meth is sometimes called the poor man's cocaine for a reason. In many respects, they are indeed similar powerful psychostimulants (National Drug Intelligence Center 2002). Users who have used both drugs report similar experiences, such as a sense of euphoria and increased alertness. Users of both drugs report experiencing an initial rush and high. If the cocaine is in crack form, the rush and high are much shorter. Users of both drugs can smoke, inject, snort, or swallow either illicit drug. Both drugs may produce anxiety, increased blood pressure, increased temperature, higher pulse rates, and possible death. Short-term effects of both include increased activity, decreased appetite, increased self-confidence, insomnia, increased pulse rate, hallucinations, grandiosity, impulsivity, irritability, confusion, anxiety, agitation, paranoia, increased libido, and increased respiration. Chronic cocaine or meth use disrupts the individual's ability to feel pleasure he or she would normally experience from positive or rewarding events. Prolonged use of either drug can lead to psychotic behaviors, hallucinations, mood disturbances, and/or violence. When users of either drug withdraw, they report cravings, paranoia, and depression (London et al. 2004). Meth users were found to have more severe psychiatric consequences than cocaine users (Rawson et al. 2000).

However, differences between the two drugs exist. Cocaine is derived from the refined leaves of the South American coca plant; consequently, almost all cocaine is imported into the United States. Most of the meth used in the United States is also imported from Mexico, Southeast Asia, and other countries. However, unlike cocaine, meth can be domestically manufactured in large or small operations. Large open spaces, while often desirable, are not required for the production of meth. Meth can be produced in small rooms or spaces, such as motel rooms, toolsheds, bedrooms, kitchens, or other small areas. The production of meth is relatively easy compared to importing cocaine. All of the necessary chemicals to produce meth are commercially available, thus making law enforcement control difficult.

Cocaine and meth abusers have different use patterns. For example, meth users typically report they use the drug on a more regular basis than that reported by cocaine users (Simon et al. 2002). Rawson et al. (2000) also found that many meth users reported daily use. Meth's effects require less frequent administration than cocaine because meth leaves the system slower and thus has a longer half-life than cocaine. Cocaine users, especially those using crack, need to administer and re-administer the drug more frequently to remain high. They report usage in the evening, and less frequently than meth users, who often use throughout the day and evening (Simon et al. 2002). Meth has a half-life of ten to twelve hours, compared with only about one hour for cocaine (Wermuth 2000). While cocaine is quickly and almost completely metabolized in the body, meth has a longer duration, and a larger percentage of the drug remains unchanged in the body (Center for Substance Abuse Prevention/ National Prevention Network 2006; National Institute on Drug Abuse 2002). Thus, the brain is affected for more prolonged spans of time. Cocaine is not neurotoxic to dopamine and serotonin neurons, but meth is neurotoxic. "Meth has more long-term, serious effects on the brain than cocaine" (National Institute on Drug Abuse 2002). In general, meth users were found to have more serious medical effects than cocaine users (Rawson et al. 2000).

Another difference is cost. Meth is cheaper on the street than cocaine. Meth has a longer duration for the initial rush and high. Crack cocaine offers a high of about 15–20 minutes and meth 8–24 hours. Cocaine users report spending more money on cocaine than meth users do on buying meth (Rawson et al. 2000; Simon et al. 2002). The perceived cost-benefit ratio to the user is much greater for the meth addict. Rawson et al. (2002, 7) wrote, "Methamphetamine effects are long lasting and methamphetamine users typically spend about 25 percent as much money for methamphetamine as that spent by cocaine users for cocaine." In addition, according to NIDA (National Institute on Drug Abuse) Director Nora Volkow (2006), amphetamines such as meth are the most potent of stimulant drugs. The result is more release of dopamine, linked to pleasure, and about three times the dopamine than cocaine.

According to research by Dr. Sara Simon, abuse patterns are different between meth and cocaine abusers (Zickler 2005a). Meth abusers typically take the drug early in the morning, in intervals of two to four hours, similar to being on a medication. In contrast, cocaine abusers typically take the drug in the evening over a period of several hours in a way that resembles a recreational use pattern. They continue using until all of the cocaine is typically gone. Another pattern was that continuous use was more common among meth abusers than those abusing cocaine. According to other NIDA-sponsored research by Dr. Simon, the effects of meth and cocaine abuse resulted in similar cognitive deficits, but meth abusers had more problems than cocaine abusers at tasks requiring attention and the ability to organize information (Zickler 2005a).

In the 1980s, cocaine use became epidemic, but in recent years has declined among the middle class. Crack cocaine remains a serious blight in some inner cities. Cocaine's use, similar to other drugs, is cyclic with periodic increases and decreases (Rawson et al. 2002). In contrast, meth has the potential of enduring, similar to marijuana and alcohol. In addition, cocaine users are also more likely to abuse alcohol, while meth users smoke marijuana (Rawson et al. 2000).

Cocaine addicts typically experience profound life changes in a relatively short time frame because of higher costs of use and use patterns, which involve binging. Cocaine users typically hit bottom sooner than many meth users. Meth addicts experience the same losses and also hit bottom but in many cases do so over a longer period of time. Some meth addicts use at levels that allow them to maintain jobs, homes, some money, or at least maintain the appearance of being in control.

LONG-TERM EFFECTS OF METH USE

Researchers have documented many of the effects of meth use, but more research is needed. Table 3.3 shows a summary of some of the short- and

Table 3.3
Summary of the Short- and Long-Term Effects of Using Methamphetamine

	Desired	Undesired
Short-Term	Feelings of pleasure	Increased pulse rate
	Sense of euphoria	Increased blood pressure
	Pain suppression	Hallucinations (auditory and visual)
	Appetite control and weight loss	Aggressive behavior
	Pain suppression	Erratic behaviors
	Escape	Bizarre behaviors
	Sense of empowerment	Increased violent behavior
	Ability to concentrate	Loss of consciousness
	Heightened sexual libido	Infections
	Sense of well-being	Delusional thinking
	Alertness	Insomnia (inability to sleep)
	Excitement	Increased body temperature
	Boredom relief	Irritability
	Talkativeness	Increased respiration
	Improved self-confidence	Confusion
	Improved self-esteem	Anxiety
	Increased activity	Death
	Ability to stay awake for prolonged periods of time	Seizures
	Perception of social acceptance	Acute psychosis
		Sores from picking at skin
Long-Term	Weight loss	Enduring psychosis and paranoia
	Escape from reality	Severe depression
	Sense of belonging to a group of "insiders"	Habitual aggressive behaviors

	Desired	Undesired
	Boredom relief	Long-term deficits in cognitive functioning
	Escape from a life of chaos	Consequences of criminal acts
	Perception of enmeshment with others	Infectious diseases
	Escape from chronic feelings of depression	Loss of pro-social associations
		Disconnection from the mainstream society
		Decreased employability
		Skin diseases and irreparable scarring
		Suicidal or homicidal thoughts
		Meth mouth—tooth decay and gum disease
		Disfiguration
		Loss of interest in sex
		Loss of interest in food, malnutrition
		Mood disturbances/ anhedonia
		Loss of ability to experience pleasure under normal circumstances
		Chronic insomnia and chronic fatigue
		Death
		Sexual dysfunction
		Seizures

Note: Data developed from the findings of several research studies on the effects of meth. These studies and sources include the American Dental Association (2005), Farrell and Marsden (2002), Greenwell and Brecht (2003), Leshner (2000), London et al. (2004), National Institutes of Health (2001, 2004), Sommers, Baskin, and Baskin-Sommers (2006), Volkow et al. (2001a, 2001b), and Wells (2006).

long-term desired and undesired effects of meth use. Some of the short-term effects continue over the long-term, whereas others become more difficult to occur, such as pleasure. The degree to which these effects occur depends on a number of factors, such as dosage amount, purity, frequency of use, amount of involvement over time, gender, age, and weight.

WHY IS METH UNIQUE?

What is so unique about meth? Meth poses unique challenges for treatment providers, counselors, and individuals trying to curb its use. Some authorities suggest that meth use and addiction are similar to other stimulants, such as cocaine, and should be addressed using the same approaches. Others conclude that meth use and addiction are unique and require special strategies. Its use does in fact pose special challenges.

One major challenge is that meth is a powerfully addictive drug. This truth poses an issue for the meth addict, family members, friends, and therapists. Some have reported that meth addiction occurred after a single use of the drug, but in reality this is rare. What is a more common pattern is that meth addiction occurs rapidly, and most addicts become addicted over a short span of time and with multiple doses.

Some users report that the drug is seductive, and they increase their use within days of their initial experience (Sommers, Baskin, and Baskin-Sommers 2006). This is attributed to the availability of the drug and desired effects, such as senses of empowerment and euphoria. It affords a strong sense of euphoria from its first use onward. Because of its effect on the user's brain and nervous system, the drug becomes almost impossible to substitute for pleasure.

Users perceive other attractive benefits beyond their being high on meth. Initial users and addicts view the drug as effective in reducing fatigue and allowing them to work for prolonged periods of time. For example, over the road, truck drivers use meth and amphetamines to stay awake on long trips. Some students view it as a study aid that allows them to study and stay focused for hours. Other individuals, especially females, view it as an effective way to lose weight. Meth metabolizes at a slower rate than many drugs, and consequently, the euphoric effects last longer for the user (Anglin et al. 2000). These positive effects of meth use, regardless of how short-term they may appear to be, are real to the user and need to be acknowledged by everyone.

Another challenge is that meth has a market that differs significantly from other drugs (Rodriguez et al. 2005). The production and distribution of the drug occurs through more informal social networks. Dealers typically only sell to people they know, and users only buy from people they know. In addition, meth is often shared among those that use. Users and producers give much of the drug away. Within the circle of users, there are generally people who will give it away to insiders and who in turn expect to get paid back when they run out and others have the drug. There is an expectation that it is given and freely exchanged among users. For example, Pennell et al. (1999) reported that among arrestees, 77 percent of meth users reported obtaining the drug for free from friends.

An additional challenge is that the drug is relatively abundant compared to illegal substances that have to be imported across national boundaries. Authorities have found labs in car trunks, mobile homes, microwave ovens, and small rooms. It is often locally produced in home laboratories using materials such as household batteries and cold medicines (Bonné 2001). Although authorities have made efforts to control the precursor chemicals used to produce meth, it is impossible to eliminate them altogether (Rawson et al. 2002). The precursor chemicals are found in multiple household products, such as cold tablets, drain cleaners, solvents, matches, and other common items. Even given some of the challenges to domestic meth production, it is important to note that most of the illegal meth used in the United States was produced in large labs in Mexico and then smuggled into the country. Federal estimates indicate that at least 80 to 90 percent of all of the illegal meth now used in the United States was produced in illegal super labs in Mexico.

The presence and prevalence of meth in rural areas represent a special challenge. Meth manufacture has been targeted in rural areas. Rural areas are attractive for dealers and manufacturers because the odors and by-products of meth production are more easily concealed from authorities. Authorities are less likely to discover meth labs located in remote rural areas. Some of the methods of production involve chemicals and substances that are associated with farming and ranching, and their possession is not viewed as extraordinary. For example, anhydrous ammonia and iodine, both chemical precursors for meth manufacture, are both commonly used on farms and ranches.

In addition to the advantages in clandestine lab production, rural areas have been hit harder with meth use than urban areas. For example, studies have shown that meth use among rural youth is higher than city youth. The decline of agriculture and the small family-owned farm, loss of jobs, decline in local economies, migration of population to the cities, sense of boredom, and remoteness (seclusion) have all promoted the use of drugs in rural areas. Given the ease of manufacture or relative availability and low cost to rural areas, inadequate law enforcement and health services, it should come as no surprise that meth would find a welcome environment. The problem becomes even more acute when faced with the reality that many rural areas lack drug treatment services. Those services available often require individuals seeking treatment to travel long distances. For many of these areas and especially rural areas, treatment is scarce to nonexistent. The unavailability of treatment programs for any form of addiction, let alone meth, in the nation's rural areas has created a treatment vacuum of national proportions.

Finally, the use of meth is not evenly distributed across the country. Meth use and manufacture can be and often are localized problems that represent another challenge. Consequently, some communities and regions are heavily impacted by the drug while others remain untouched. Western and southern states, and more specifically rural areas, have been particularly hard hit by meth use. With its presence differing from locality to locality, it is difficult for some communities to support regional or statewide prevention and treatment responses. Part of the difficulty at the national level has been to get regions of the country not severely impacted by meth, such as the northeastern states, on board with a coordinated and national response to the meth problem. Consequently, only recently have national leaders been concerned with the meth problem.

IMPLICATIONS FOR TREATMENT

Compared to other drugs, meth does have a different effect on users. This fact has led some to conclude that treatment for meth addiction must be unique. However, a considerable amount of evidence suggests that many of the treatment approaches for cocaine addiction are equally appropriate for meth dependency (Rawson et al. 2000). Many of these approaches will be of benefit to most meth-dependent clients, but any treatment approach will need to be modified to the special needs of meth addicts.

Without question, meth has significant cognitive impacts on the meth-dependent user. A number of researchers have found evidence that the brains of chronic meth users look similar to patients with Parkinson's disease. Individuals addicted to meth may experience high levels of paranoia, anxiety, lack of focus, and attention span difficulties. Asking for help is difficult for any addiction, and meth is no exception. In addition, meth addiction is similar to any other in that the addict initially finds it difficult to admit he or she is an addict.

Prolonged use of meth causes physical damage to the brain, which alters its ability to function. In short, the brain will need time to heal. Researchers across the country are trying to better understand how the brain is damaged and whether it will repair itself over time. So far, the results suggest that much of the damage to the brain can heal. Some authorities have concluded that the health effects of meth use need to be understood to more effectively provide treatment (Greenwell and Brecht 2003). For example, given the effects of prolonged use on brain functioning and short-term memory, treatment information must be simple, or easy to understand, and should be repeated. This is due partially to the negative effect meth has on the reasoning portion of the brain. Meth addicts struggle often with sequential thinking and instructions.

Chronic meth use disrupts the individual's ability to feel pleasure he or she would normally experience from positive or rewarding experiences. Prolonged meth use, like that of cocaine, reduces the user's ability to experience pleasure through the dopamine pathways. This poses a challenge for treatment approaches that rely exclusively on rewards for compliance. The implication for treatment is that rewards that are simple and frequent are more likely to be effective than those that are few and far between. What rewards are used must be valued by the client and bring pleasure.

Many meth addicts come from environments in which violence was common. Some meth addicts may become more violent, and some are often the victims of violence. In one study of meth users, the researchers found reports of violence and abuse were "extensive" (Cohen et al. 2003). The therapist needs to consider this when thinking about treatment and recovery. For females, many have been subjected to sexual abuse, domestic violence, emotional abuse, and mistreatment. They most often experience this violence through interpersonal relationships, usually with males (Cohen et al. 2003). For men, many have been victims of violence from other males. Regardless, it important for the therapist to acknowledge in treatment that violence may be part of the equation and PTSD (post-traumatic stress disorder) may be present. Cohen et al. (2003) recommend that it is imperative that when indicated, the treatment for violence and PTSD be addressed.

In addition, the depression associated with long-term withdrawal must be addressed. Meth users trying to abstain from use may experience anxiety, fatigue, paranoia, aggression, and depression (Katsumata, Sato, and Kashiwade 1993). Volkow (2006) told Congress that brain scan research is showing that the brains of meth addicts in withdrawal resemble the brains of clinically depressed patients. Aware of the depression, physicians are prescribing antidepressants, such as Welbutrin (bupropion), to help those in withdrawal deal with their chronic depression and subsequent cravings for meth.

In addition, meth users in recovery, similar to others with drug dependence issues, can be triggered by psychological, sociological, and environmental stimuli. A simple trip to the pharmacy or grocery store may trigger cravings for the drug during the recovery process. When the authors make presentations on meth, they always advise the audience of video clips involving needles and other triggers for those in recovery. Meth addicts face another challenge, which treatment experts label the "wall." Typically, around 45–120 days into recovery, meth addicts experience physiological changes that may lead to a relapse to meth use. The "wall" is a period in which the addict experiences severe depression and craves the drug that he or she believes will cure the depression. The "wall" is often touted by pessimists as one of the main reasons why addicts fail in treatment. While the "wall" cannot be ignored, it is possible to climb over the wall and have full recovery.

Meth addicts in treatment are dealing with altered brains (Volkow 2006). They have distorted thinking patterns and delusions. Their needs and desires are rearranged in a hierarchy different from what they were when they first started use. Basic needs, such as for sleep, safety, and food have been supplanted with their addiction to meth. The meth moves to or near the top of their hierarchy of needs. Thus, they crave the drug and can easily be triggered to its use. They chose meth over taking care of themselves.

The distribution of meth is different from that of other illegal substances. It is not generally a street drug but is sold or provided by family, friends, and associates. For example, in a small interview-based study of street youth, most of those using meth reported they were given it for free from friends (Bungay et al. 2006). This makes law enforcement activities challenging, as the drug is less on the street than marijuana, heroin, cocaine, and other street drugs.

ROUTES OF ADMINISTRATION AND INFECTIOUS DISEASES

Meth users can inject, smoke, swallow, anally or vaginally insert, or snort meth. The method the user selects influences how the drug is experienced. Meth is a bitter-tasting powder that easily dissolves in beverages. The powder form of the drug is often snorted, which produces a less intense but much longer-lasting high. In 1993, 42 percent of meth and amphetamine treatment admissions reported they used the drug in this manner, according to the Substance Abuse and Mental Health Services Administration (SAMHSA 2006). By 2003, only 15 percent of the treatment admissions reported they snorted/inhaled the drug. Recent TEDS (Treatment Episode Data Set) data found that in 2003, 56 percent of primary meth and amphetamine admissions reported smoking the drug, which was up from the 15 percent reported in 1993 (SAMHSA 2006). Many studies have confirmed that smoking meth is the most common way it is used. In 1993, 29 percent indicated they injected the drug, which compares to 22 percent in 2003. Smoking or injecting the drug produces a short but more intense and pleasurable "rush." In 1993, oral ingestion represented 13 percent, and "other," 1 percent of the routes of administration. By 2003, oral administration declined to 6 percent, and "other" routes of administration remained unchanged at 1 percent (SAMHSA 2006).

Powdered meth is a hydrochloride salt form, which absorbs water from the air quickly. This form of meth is smokeable, as is "crystal meth" or "ice," which refers to meth grown into crystals. Although some people believe that crystal meth is a freebase form of meth, this is not true. Meth that is grown into crystals is simply easier to smoke. Meth in crystal form, rather than powder, also is more likely to be relatively pure because of the difficulty of growing crystals from impure chemicals. Individuals absorb crystal meth differently and report different experiences when they are high (Lee 2006).

According to SAMHSA (2004) in 1992, 12 percent of meth and amphetamine treatment admissions reported they smoked meth. By 2002, 50 percent of the treatment admissions for meth reported they smoked it in its crystal form. This represents a major shift from inhaling to smoking meth over this 10-year span. This shift to smoking is likely due to the advantages smoking offers to the user, which is a more efficient way to absorb the drug. The lungs are very efficient in absorbing meth rather than the nose and the effects are stronger and quicker than snorting. A downside is that, contrary to popular belief, smoking is almost as addicting as injecting the drug.

Another method of consuming meth is called "booty bumping" or "blasting." This process involves the user's heating meth into liquid form and mixing it with water. The user then draws the fluid into a syringe that lacks a needle. The syringe is then inserted in the anus and meth shot into the user's body. Users rely on this technique because the drug is readily absorbed into the bloodstream. This form of administration offers advantages to gay men, because meth constricts blood vessels in the rectum and consequently makes anal intercourse less painful for the receiving partner. The downside is that tears and damage to the lining of the rectum increases the risk of sexually transmitted diseases, such as HIV, entering the bloodstream.

Another new way to use meth is called "parachuting," which involves the user wrapping meth in a paper and letting the drug slowly release as the paper unwraps in the digestive system (Hendrickson et al. 2006). It is a method where the user attempts to prolong the duration of the drug. "Parachuting" is a known method of administration in some drug circles with other drugs, such as ecstasy or heroin. This method of administration may result in a delayed toxic response for the user.

The crystal form of meth is referred to as "crystal," "ice," or "glass." If heat is introduced, the user can smoke or inject crystal meth. The user finds that smoking it is a much faster, and more intense, high than swallowing the drug. The user places a small amount of crystal in a glass pipe (often called a tooter), heats it, and inhales the resulting vapors. Crystal meth, or ice, melts into a liquid when heated and returns to its crystal form when cooled. Boiling crystal turns it into a semiliquid referred to as snot, which can be smoked or placed up the nose. Users view smoking meth as ideal because it can be used almost anywhere since the vapors are odorless and undetectable.

The rush or high felt by the user is the direct result of the release of dopamine into the section of the brain that controls feelings of pleasure. If it is snorted, the user usually experiences effects within about five minutes. If it is orally ingested, the user will feel a rush in around 20 minutes. Oral meth use tends to lack rushing, has less euphoric effects, and tends to cause far less of a feeling of wanting to do it again than the other methods.

When the user smokes or injects meth, the fastest rush results. The user usually experiences an immediate and powerful response. Smoking and injecting are associated with stronger, faster, and more euphoric effects. While injecting results in a faster reward, it also results in a faster crash. Users learn to manage the rapid crashes by trying to attain another rush by taking more of the drug. These effects are more associated with compulsive/addictive user patterns. The general trend is toward smoking meth because of this immediacy and strength of the initial rush. It should be noted that many addicts have an aversion to using needles and never inject the drug. In addition, smoking meth is almost as addictive as injecting the drug.

Regardless of the method of use, meth addicts will frequently use it with other drugs such as cocaine, marijuana, and alcohol. Because of their polydrug use, it is sometimes difficult to sort out the effects of the meth from those of other drugs. Users rely on other drugs or alcohol to either enhance or supplement the meth high or cushion their withdrawal and depression when coming down. Another common element of meth use is that users often construct their settings to accommodate the effects of the drug, such as adjusting the lighting and playing certain music (Lovett 1994).

WHO IS USING METHAMPHETAMINE?

What populations are more likely to use meth? Summarizing the literature Wermuth (2000, 423) wrote, "Low-income and unemployed young white men continue to be the group most likely to use meth, but by the mid-1990s the drug had increased in popularity in more diverse populations and regions." Numerous studies have found that meth use is predominantly a White phenomenon (Anglin et al. 2000; Yacoubian and Peters 2004; Zule and Desmond 1999). During the 1990s, meth was essentially used by white males between the ages of 18 and 35 years (Rodriguez et al. 2005). In 1992, 62 percent of treatment admissions were White. Whites increased to 66 percent of the admissions in 2002. A SAMHSA Report (2005b) estimated a prevalence of about 0.7 percent for Whites. According to SAMHSA's (2005c) *The DASIS Report*, January 7, 2005, treatment admissions for methamphetamine or amphetamine abuse in 1992 were 55 percent male, which remained stable through 2002. The mean age for treatment admissions increased over this period to 29 years in 2002. Of those being admitted for treatment, 25 percent indicated they had part-time or full-time jobs.

However, meth users come from a wide variety of socioeconomic profiles. The penetration of meth into other demographic circles is occurring. For example, a Sacramento, California study found that users came from all walks of life and some users started in their teens (Gibson, Leamon, and Flynn 2002). Anglin and Rawson (1998) reported other groups, such as Latinos, gay-bisexual males, older adult arrestees, and adolescents were increasingly involved. Outlining the extent of the problem, Kathy Jett during a February 2006 briefing of Capitol Hill staff and National Association of Counties shared that meth use by Hispanic women was a fast-growing problem in California. In a similar vein, Joe (1996) found and reported on meth abuse among Asian-Pacific women in Honolulu, San Francisco, and San Diego. In addition, there are numerous anecdotal reports on the broad spectrum of users, such as high-achieving students, who use the drug to perform better in school and college, and others such as athletes, cheerleaders, beauty pageant participants, and models to improve performance (Rawson et al. 2002). While many are at risk of meth addiction, some populations identified in the literature are of special concern.

In one of the larger studies of meth use, Oetting et al. (2000) reviewed data from over 600,000 students and found that female meth use had increased dramatically but males remained the predominant users. Many females battle body image issues and the cultural pressures to be thin. The relationship between females and meth use for weight control is well documented in the literature. Meth use does result in easy, rapid, and inexpensive weight loss. Women, more than men, report they use meth to lose weight. Women are more likely than men to also experience low self-esteem and lower self-confidence. Meth users, at least initially, boast their self-esteem and self-confidence. Meth addiction and treatment admissions for women are proportionately higher than for other illegal substances, such as heroin or cocaine.

Females who have emotional relationships with males who are addicted to meth are another population of users. The males encourage and often demand of the females in their lives also to use meth in order to "bond" with them. If the male is using, it is likely the female is also using. Anecdotally, a common pattern is for an older male to introduce and encourage the use of meth to a younger female. The older males typically promise to provide good meth and protect them from harm when they are high or crashing from meth use. Another group, usually female, consists of stay-at-home adults, who begin using meth for its short-term benefits, such as its energy boost, treatment of depression, and related weight loss (Rawson 2005).

Workaholics or low-income adults also use meth to stay awake and perform in multiple jobs. Working low-income individuals find meth attractive because they must work several jobs or long hours to support themselves or their families. They find the higher energy and alertness (ability to stay awake for prolonged periods) help them cope with the demands of multiple jobs for economic reasons. Probably the best example of this are over-the-road truckers, some of whom use meth (or amphetamine), allowing them to keep driving long distances.

Rural residents interested in manufacturing meth for profit and personal use are another group at risk of involvement with meth. Meth is considered by some to be a response to the "plight of the weary." Meth is particularly attractive in rural areas where farming and the economy are in decline. Some rural residents view the production, sales, and use of meth an attractive alternative to unemployment or financial hardship (Wermuth 2000). For example, North Carolina profiled the typical user as, "young, white, small-town residents with limited education and a blue collar-career" (North Carolina Division of Social Services and the Family and Children's Resource Program 2005). A study that compared rural with urban illegal substance use in Nebraska found that while illegal use was prevalent in urban Omaha, meth use was more common in rural areas (Herz 2000).

Rural youth engaged in substance abuse also find meth attractive. Spoth et al. (2006, 876) wrote, "Adolescents in smaller towns and rural areas are particularly vulnerable, given potentially powerful peer influences in rural environments and the historical appeal of stimulants to rural youth." Another study found that rural and small-town youth were more likely than their urban counterparts to become substance abusers (National Center on Addiction and Substance Abuse at Columbia University 2000). The same report found that rural eighth graders were 104 percent more likely than urban eighth graders to use amphetamines. This same group was 59 percent more likely to use methamphetamine than urban eighth graders. In summary, marginalized rural youth who have been touched by economic downturns in their local economies have a greater likelihood of being involved with meth.

However, meth use is not restricted to rural youth. Youth from a variety of urban settings also use the drug. For example, researchers found meth use among homeless youth who lived on the streets of Vancouver (Bungay et al. 2006) and San Francisco (Auerswald and Eyre 2002). In these studies, researchers found that street youth used meth to stay awake while they were on the streets, increase sexual performance, and control hunger pain between sporadic and infrequent meals.

The gay community has been particularly hard hit by the use of meth. Use of meth at circuit parties, nightclubs, bars, and gathering places of gay men has been disproportionately high. Meth use, especially crystal meth, has become very much part of the gay identity in some gay communities (Reback and Grella 1999), with meth being the drug of choice. Some gay men use meth to enhance their sexual experiences and stimulate sexual behavior. Gay men who are interested in increased sexual activity and performance have found meth to be the ideal drug. According to Freese et al. (2000), urban gay males living along the West Coast of California represent a large segment of the meth-using population. Lee (2006) reported that about 11 percent of meth users are gay men and use reaches 20 percent in some gay communities. The user's sense of euphoria from using the drug reduces normal inhibitions about sex and multiple partners.

Heterosexuals drawn to sexual experimentation and sexual experiences use the drug to alter their sexual pleasure (Wermuth 2000). Meth is known to lower sexual inhibitions, making it attractive to those interested in sexual activity and seduction. The desired effects of meth and corresponding sexual libido make meth an attractive drug to enhance sexual encounters. Research on the relationship between meth use and sexual behavior has confirmed that chronic meth users tend to have more sexual partners, sell sex for money or drugs, and take more sexual risks than nonusers (Kall 1992; Molitor et al. 1999).

Some Native Americans are meth users, including those living on reservations. Native American meth use is spreading across the reservations. Faced with high unemployment, alcoholism, mental issues, domestic violence, and few prospects, many Native Americans turn to meth as a cheap and powerful relief to their situation. In a special *Newsweek* report, journalist Andrew Murr (2004) found that meth was becoming a "scourge" affecting Native Americans living on reservations. The SAMHSA (2005b) estimates the prevalence of meth use among Native Americans and Alaska Natives at about 1.7 percent. Freese et al. (2000) summarized the literature and noted that new approaches need to be designed to address the meth problem in Native American communities. They noted that Native American communities in South Dakota,

Wyoming, and Montana are moving forward in addressing the problem at the community level. Tribal groups, such as the Chippewa Cree, Crow, Flathead, Lakota, Navaho, Northern Cheyenne, Washoe, and Yavapai, to name a few, have identified meth as a problem among their peoples.

It is evident that the demographic profile of meth users is changing. The Administrator of SAMHSA, Charles Currie, provided congressional testimony that meth use was "...expanding to Hispanic and Asian populations, and tribal leaders are reporting increased use of methamphetamines by Native Americans" (Currie 2005, 2). In California, he shared that meth use is on the rise for Hispanic women. He also noted the increased vulnerability and use by the 18- to 25-year-old population. Other evidence indicates that meth use has the potential to spread to other populations. Rawson et al. wrote:

> Meth use is expanding from a purely Caucasian, English-speaking clientele to Hispanic and Asian populations. Although the use of methamphetamine appears to be minimal among African Americans, increases among Hispanics and Asians suggest expansion of the methamphetamine problem to new markets. (Rawson et al. 2002, 8)

Astounding as it sounds, there are even anecdotal reports of meth making inroads into Mormon and Amish communities (Lee 2006). Whether meth spreads to new ethnic and cultural groups remains to be seen. Some research has found that strong ethnic identification and segregation may offset some drug risks (Zickler 2005b). For example, meth use has not made serious inroads into the African American population.

HOW MUCH USE IS OCCURRING?

Meth is a growing worldwide problem (Farrell and Marsden 2002). The World Health Organization estimated that over 35 million individuals use meth on a regular basis, which is more than the combined total of estimated cocaine users (15 million) and heroin users (less than 10 million) (United Nations Office for Drug Control and Crime Prevention 2006). In the United States, a number of national efforts are made to track the extent of drug use, treatment, production, arrests, and other data. These data are useful in identifying trends.

SELF-REPORTED METH USE BY STUDENTS

One of the most widely known studies on substance use is the MTF (Monitoring the Future) survey. This study is an annual national survey that assesses the beliefs, attitudes, and behaviors of high school students in grades

8, 10, and 12, as well as young adults. The study does not include school dropouts, which could represent a high-risk group for meth use. A serious limitation of this and similar studies is that it excludes school dropouts and other high-risk youth, such as those living on the streets. The MTF study surveys about 50,000 subjects. Since 1999, meth has been included in the survey. Table 3.4 shows that meth use is not common among high-school-aged youth. The numbers are low, which is encouraging. However, before becoming too optimistic, one must realize the usage reported is at least three years old and does not capture recent regional expansion of the drug.

The Monitoring the Future study also presents data on a sample of young adults, which shed light on the prevalence of meth use. Graph 3.1 shows the percentage of young adults in the sample that reported some use of meth over their lifetimes. The graph also reveals that self-reported meth use hovers close to 8 percent for this population. This does not mean that these young adults continue to use meth but only that they have at least tried it and still may be using it.

METH USERS WHO COME TO HOSPITAL EMERGENCY DEPARTMENTS

Drug-related emergency department mentions are provided by the SAMHSA through its Drug Abuse Warning Network, referred to by the acronym DAWN. DAWN provides national information on morbidity and mortalities related to substance abuse, including meth's, collected from short-stay medical and medical examiner offices across the United States. The DAWN study is an annual survey of emergency department episodes from metropolitan areas, which is useful in understanding meth and other substance abuse patterns. The DAWN data show that meth-related deaths and emergency department episodes have increased in many urban areas over recent years. For example, in 2005, according to the DAWN data, meth was involved in 108,905 emergency room visits (SAMHSA 2006). Graph 3.2 illustrates the increase in emergency department visits for methamphetamine from 1995 to 2005. The data show that emergency department meth mentions have increased by 583.5 percent from 15,933 in 1995 to 108,905 in 2005. Clearly, dramatically more meth-using people found their way into America's emergency rooms over this 10-year span. There may be several reasons for this increase, including the increase in overdoses due to higher purity of the drug on the streets. In addition, possible increased use, awareness, and sensitivity by emergency room staff, and individual willingness to seek help may all play roles in explaining more reported emergency episodes.

Table 3.4
Percentage of Methamphetamine Use among Secondary School Students by Grade, 1999–2005

Lifetime							
Grade	1999	2000	2001	2002	2003	2004	2005
8th	4.5%	4.2%	4.4%	3.5%	3.9%	2.5%	3.1%
10th	7.3	6.9	6.4	6.1	5.2	5.3	4.1
12th	8.2	7.9	6.9	6.7	6.2	6.2	4.5
Annual							
Grade	1999	2000	2001	2002	2003	2004	2005
8th	3.2%	2.5%	2.8%	2.2%	2.5%	1.5%	1.8%
10th	4.6	4.0	3.7	6.1	3.3	3.0	2.9
12th	4.7	4.3	3.9	6.7	3.2	3.4	2.5
Past 30 days							
Grade	1999	2000	2001	2002	2003	2004	2005
8th	1.1%	0.8%	1.3%	1.1%	1.2%	0.6%	0.7%
10th	1.8	2.0	1.5	1.8	1.4	1.3	1.1
12th	1.7	1.9	1.5	1.7	1.7	1.4	0.9

Source: National Institute on Drug Abuse, Monitoring the Future Study, 2005.

TREATMENT ADMISSIONS FOR METH

The TEDS, once labeled the Client Data System, collects data on demographic and substance abuse characteristics of admissions to facilities that receive state substance abuse funds. TEDS is an annual compilation of data on the demographic characteristics and substance abuse problems of those admitted for substance abuse treatment. In 1992–1993, with 42 states and the District of Columbia reporting, admissions due to meth abuse increased in 23 out of 29 reporting states for a net increase of 43 percent (Wermuth 2000). Meth was the primary substances of abuse in over 116,595 substance abuse treatment admissions in 2003, as reported to TEDS (SAMHSA 2005a). In comparison, the same TEDS data showed that the number of meth admissions for 1993 was 20,776, which indicates admissions increased

Graph 3.1
Trends in Lifetime Prevalence of Use of Methamphetamine for Young Adults (19–28)

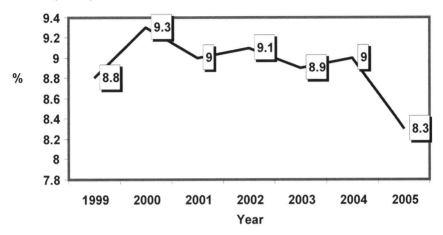

Source: National Institute on Drug Abuse, Monitoring the Future Study, 2005.

Graph 3.2
Number of Emergency Department Visits for Methamphetamine, 1995–2005

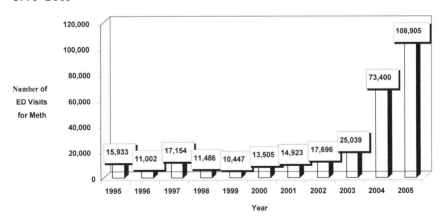

Source: Substance Abuse and Mental Health Services Administration—Drug Abuse Warning Network, 2006.

by 461 percent over this 10-year span. The SAMHSA (2005a) reported that from 1992 to 2002 the amphetamine and meth treatment admission rate in the United States increased from 10 to 52 per 100,000 over this 10-year span. In California, a state at the forefront of meth use and manufacture, publicly funded meth treatment increased 226 percent from 1992 to 1998 (Brecht 2001). In the state of Washington, treatment admissions increased more than 1,000 percent from 1992 to the first half of 1998 (Mills 1999). Nationally, this trend continued as reported admissions to publicly funded treatment for meth abuse grew from 12,122 in 1992 to 55,582 in 2002, representing more than a fourfold increase (Hser, Evans, and Huang 2005). This may be reflective of increased interest by meth addicts in getting treatment and/or more court-ordered treatment for meth.

The DASIS Report, March 15, 2006, of SAMHSA summarized that meth and amphetamine were identified in more than 136,000 cases as the primary substance of abuse in treatment admissions. This represented about 7 percent of all treatment admissions. The same report noted that between 1993 and 2003, the meth and/or amphetamine admission rate increased from 13 to 56 admissions per 100,000 population aged 12 years or older. This represents a 330 percent increase over the period. The report concluded that 18 states had meth and/or amphetamine treatment rates that were higher than the national average of 56 per 100,000 population 12 years or older. In addition the report found, "The proportion of primary methamphetamine/amphetamine admissions referred to treatment by the criminal justice system increased from 36 percent in 1993 to 51 percent in 2003." This later conclusion indicates methamphetamine and amphetamine users more frequently are being ordered by the courts into treatment.

SELF-REPORTED USE BY AGE

Another way to measure substance use is to survey a sample of households. The National Household Survey on Drug Abuse is an annual national survey of drug use by household. During the year 2000, the Drug Enforcement Administration found that 4 percent of the U.S. population reported trying meth at some time over their lifetime (SAMHSA 2001). According to its 2004 survey, about 12 million people aged 12 and older reported they had used meth at least once in their lifetime. These people represent about 5.3 percent of the total population. The percentages of reported use from the 2004 household survey broken down by age are shown in table 3.5.

It should be noted that a higher treatment rate is not proof that the number of meth users or the prevalence of meth abuse is increasing. Rather, it is an

Table 3.5
Percentage of Lifetime Methamphetamine Use among U.S. Population by
Age Group, 2004

Age group	Percent reporting having used meth in their lifetime	Percent reporting having used meth during the past year	Percent reporting having used meth during the past month
12 and over	4.9	0.6	0.2
12–17	1.2	0.6	0.2
18–25	5.2	1.6	0.6
26 and older	5.3	0.4	0.2

Source: Substance Abuse and Mental Health Services Administration, National Survey on Drug Use and Health, 2005.

indicator that more people are seeking or have been ordered into treatment. In addition, meth users have differing degrees of involvement with the drug. Some only occasionally use and might be considered recreational users, others use it on a routine basis, and some of these users binge on the drug and seldom ever go off of the drug. When they do come off meth, they crash and feel miserable.

METH TREATMENT

Compared to other chronic illnesses, addictions are highly treatable. O'Brien and McLellan (1996) in a review of treatment research found that for alcoholism treatment success rates averaged about 50 percent (range 40–70 percent, opiate dependence 60 percent (range 50–80 percent), cocaine dependence 55 percent (range 50–60 percent), and nicotine dependence 30 percent (range 20–40 percent). One of the major myths is that treatment does not work when it comes to meth addiction. This myth has been fuelled partially by the media and the absence of systematic research on meth treatment modalities. Little systematic research has been conducted on the efficacy of treatment for or prevention of meth addiction, but this is beginning to change. The Matrix model for treating stimulant abuse is the most frequently cited systematic research. The literature has also supported cognitive-behavioral approaches in treating meth and other addictions.

This is not to suggest that general data on meth treatment is not available. In congressional testimony, the Executive Director of NASADAD

(Gallant 2006, 2) shared data from three states that supported services for meth addiction:

- In Colorado, 80 percent of methamphetamine users were abstinent at discharge in FY 2003;

- In Iowa, a 2003 study found that 71.2 percent of methamphetamine users were abstinent and 90.4 percent had not been arrested six months after treatment; and

- In Tennessee, over 65 percent of methamphetamine users were abstinent six months after treatment.

METH TREATMENT APPROACHES
THAT HAVE PROMISE

Researchers have studied a variety of treatment approaches to stimulants, usually cocaine, and specifically meth addiction. Because they are both powerful stimulants, research on the efficacy of cocaine treatments can shed light on treating meth use and addiction. According to Dr. Nora Volkow (2006), the most effective treatments for meth addiction are behavioral therapies. Volkow also indicated that behavioral therapies are most effective when coupled with medications. The appendix contains a set of technical tables that summarize a sample of studies that have researched the effectiveness of some of the main treatment approaches to stimulant, mostly cocaine and meth. They are representative of what some of evidence-based practice shows are effective in treating stimulant and specifically meth use. Some of the most common treatment approaches are:

Cognitive-behavioral therapy (CBT). Several cognitive-behavioral interventions designed to help modify a patient's thinking and behaviors, and to increase skills in coping with various life stresses, have been found to be effective. Bux and Irwin (2006, 144) described the cognitive-behavioral model as follows:

> According to the cognitive behavioral model of addiction and recovery, there are three key factors that mediate recovery from substance abuse: motivation or readiness for change, self-efficacy, that is, the individual's estimation of the likelihood that he or she will succeed in changing should he or she decide to do so, and the development and successful implementation of skills for coping with the temptation to use. Consequently, treatment itself is likely to comprise two primary sets of strategies: motivation enhancement, and skills training.

Participants in CBT analyze situations and emotions that are linked to relapse and then practice ways to manage craving. Substance users learn to identify and correct problematic behaviors. Abstinence is demystified and made to be more realistic. According to NIDA (2006), cognitive-behavioral approaches can be helpful for many patients in stopping drug use and can complement other treatments. NIDA also notes that cognitive-behavioral approaches can help motivate patients to stay in treatment, take medications, learn strategies to avoid relapse, and lead drug-free lives. Cognitive-behavioral approaches result in changes that last months after treatment. Often cognitive-behavioral approaches are combined with medications for treatment.

Cognitive-behavioral approaches have been combined with giving patients vouchers (see contingency management) when patients submit drug-free urine samples and/or comply with treatment. These vouchers may be used to acquire desired items and services such as food, clothing, entertainment, special privileges, and other benefits.

Contingency management (CM) or motivational incentives. CM approaches reward patients meeting substance abuse treatment objectives. CM is "...the systematic reinforcement of desired behaviors and the withholding of reinforcement or punishment of undesired behaviors" (Higgins and Petry 1999, 122). CM basically consists of a system of positive and negative reinforcers designed to make continued substance abuse unattractive and abstinence more attractive. CM employs rules and positive or negative consequences to help patients change their behavior. A typical rule would be that the patient should provide substance-free urine samples.

CM approaches have generally demonstrated effectiveness in treating cocaine dependence in clinical trials across the country (see appendix). There is considerable evidence that CM and its similar approaches are effective in treating substance abuse disorders. Typically, CM quickly reduced cocaine use, but effects were reduced following treatment. The National Institute on Drug Abuse (2006) recently reported on research that CM coupled with psychosocial therapy was more effective in treating meth addiction than psychosocial therapy alone.

How reinforcements are administered is a critical aspect to CM. According to some authorities who use CM, there are basic principles for reinforcement (Kellogg et al. 2005). Some of these principles of reinforcement are that it should be very frequent and easy to accomplish, and rewards need to be material and services valued by the patients and connected to specific desired behaviors. In addition, therapists should focus on positive and not negative behaviors.

The main criticism leveled at CM has been the cost associated with providing rewards to patients for treatment compliance. Several research studies by

Nancy Petry and others (Jang and Schoppelrey 2005) have illustrated that low-cost CM can be very effective while keeping costs to a manageable level. The costs of CM should always be weighed against the social cost of continued meth use and addiction. For example, the cost of placing a child in foster care because of parental addiction to meth is much higher, financially and emotionally, than adequately treating the parent(s).

Motivational incentives for enhancing drug abuse recovery. This approach uses incentives to help cocaine- and meth-addicted patients with their abstinence. Initial results from NIDA's clinical trials network indicate that those receiving incentives were twice more likely to achieve eight weeks of abstinence than the control group.

Motivational enhancement therapy (MET). MET attempts to draw from the patient his or her own motivation for wanting to change and consolidating planned reasons into a plan to achieve that change. This approach centers on the client and identifies discrepancies between the patient's perceptions of current behavior and goals. The approach assumes that intrinsic motivation is a necessary and sometimes sufficient condition for patient change.

Matrix model. The Matrix model of treatment combines CM with CBT and family education for a 16-week period. The Matrix model is the most widely recognized stimulant treatment approach in the United States. It is both an individual- and group-based treatment program. Developed by Richard Rawson and his colleagues at University of California, Los Angeles, the Matrix model provides rewards to patients with clean urine samples who attend their treatment sessions. It includes components that address relapse prevention, behavioral changes, family communication, healthy environments, and other subjects important to avoiding meth use. The Matrix model is one of the most thoroughly documented and investigated approaches that have been shown to be effective in treating addiction to stimulants.

Medications. According to NIDA, there are currently no medications available to treat addiction to or overdose of amphetamine or amphetamine-like drugs, such as meth. Researchers at NIDA are working to identify chemical compounds that alter the effects of psychostimulants, such as cocaine and meth, on behavior and the brain (NIDA 2006). Patients in recovery may experience irritability and depression, and be psychotic.

Because severe depression is often characteristic of withdrawal, some patients may need antidepressant and antipsychotic medications in recovery. Antidepressant medications can be prescribed to combat the depressive symptoms frequently seen in methamphetamine withdrawal. In 2000, NIDA conducted a think tank on meth addiction, which encouraged research on medications that could treat meth overdose, improve cognitive skills, reverse impairments, and treat associated psychoses (NIDA 2005a). Some of the medications NIDA is studying include Bupropion (Welbutrin), Sertraline, Lobeline, Ariprazole, Clonidine, Modafinil (used to treat narcolepsy), Preindopril, Rivastigmine, Topiramate, Sabril or Vigabatrin, and Baclofen. A clinical trial of an antiepileptic medication labeled Topamax has shown some promising results (Volkow 2006).

Motivational interviewing. Motivational interviewing holds that clients (addicts) are the ones responsible for making decisions about making change and are the agent for change. The goals for change (reduced use) rest with the addict. Many addicts enter treatment somewhat ambivalent about changing their behavior, which may be especially true of meth addicts (Bux and Irwin 2006). Addicts decide what is reasonable, given his or her addiction, and then set out with the help of the therapist to accomplish those goals. Therapists using motivational interviewing rely on open-ended questions, affirmations, reflective listening, and summary statements. These are known under the acronym of OARS. Evidence suggests that motivational interventions typically result in positive behavioral changes, including decreased substance abuse. While motivational interviewing appears to work for many, it is not fully understood how it works (Nahom 2005).

Motivational interviewing needs to acknowledge that while addicts have reasons for quitting substance use, they may also have powerful reasons for continuing to use. This is particularly true of meth addicts (Bux and Irwin 2006). Effective therapists using this approach must avoid discounting these reasons for continued use and strategize on how to address these motivations in other ways. Confrontation is avoided so as not to stifle the addict's exploration of use rather than put them on the defensive. Motivational interviewing involves a sense of empathy between the therapist and the addict. While the therapist may not approve of use, it is still important to understand the behavior.

OTHER APPROACHES

Other substance abuse approaches include 12-step programs, which historically have focused on alcoholism and, to a lesser degree, on narcotics. If a 12-step program is used for meth addiction, it is usually in conjunction with other therapeutic approaches. For example, the Matrix model incorporates a 12-step component into its approach.

Steven Lee, MD, in his book *Overcoming Crystal Meth Addiction* (2006) offers a five-component approach to meth addiction. He writes for a broad audience but directs many of his comments to the addict on a personal level.

Dr. Lee's approach is essentially one of harm reduction, or less use is better. He recommends these to the meth addict:

- Learn as much as you can.
- Take a close look at what role crystal plays in your life.
- Learn the basic steps to stop using crystal.
- Learn how to stay clean.
- Make sure that you address major "holes" in your life that you may be trying to fill with crystal: depression, loneliness, weight control, boredom, sexual excitement, low self-esteem.

Others suggest that meth addicts must spend time in confinement, at least until they detoxify. They contend that treatment will not be of any value until addicts are free from the effects of the meth. Plus, they argue, it is less costly to confine them for a short period than treat them. Only when they have been free from the drug for awhile, does it make sense to treat them. In Minnesota, a meth boot camp operates in a similar fashion over a six-month period, where efforts are made to detoxify the meth addict and run the individual through a highly structured program of exercise, literacy, drug treatment, military drills, and other classes before reintroducing the client back into the community (Prah 2005).

THE EFFECTIVENESS OF METH TREATMENT

The proverbial elephant in the room is, "Does treatment work and for whom does it work?" The media and general public often assume, given meth's powerful addictive properties, that anyone using the drug on a regular basis is almost hopelessly addicted. Several myths about the effectiveness of treatment have shaped public opinion about treatment, and continue to do so. This runs contrary to what we know from research. Yes, meth addition is powerful and can be all encompassing in the user's life, but there is persuasive evidence that treatment can work for most. NIDA has concluded that the most effective treatments are cognitive-behavioral interventions that teach the addict to think and act differently; addressing life's stressors more effectively. What does not work is simple detoxification over a period of time, nor do confrontational approaches. Specifically, forcing the meth addict to break through denial may result in a violent response.

Based on an extensive review of the literature, it is clear that some approaches work better than others and that no one approach represents the proverbial "silver bullet," otherwise known as the cure-all for meth addiction. Typically, treatment does not have the success rates of modified approaches, such as what is known as the Matrix model. It is possible to pull out of the research some basic characteristics of approaches that work.

Community-based approaches fare better than simple individually focused treatment. Meth is a community problem, and the community needs to wrap around the meth addict's needs. In addition, successful treatments always involve cognitive-behavioral components. CBT focuses on how the way we think affects our behavior, feelings, and actions. CBT identifies and helps the individual plan for responses to triggers. These plans need to be for the long term, as recovery is a long process.

Successful treatments are highly structured, as the addict needs to replace the chaos that has been the lifestyle for the addict before entering treatment. The more structured the approach, the less time the addict has to think about using the drug. The recovering meth addict needs to have frequent contact with the treatment providers. They also need to be held accountable for their behaviors in relationship to the drug.

Successful treatment needs to address medical, nutritional, and mental health issues that may have resulted from prolonged meth use. For example, meth addicts typically do not eat well, nor do they feel good about themselves when they are not using the substance. These and other issues need to be addressed in a holistic manner. Another dimension that needs to be addressed for some in treatment may be sexually transmitted diseases, such as HIV and the corresponding AIDS.

CHAPTER 4

Effective Community-Based Treatment for Methamphetamine Addiction

COMMUNITIES

The topic of this book is treatment of meth addiction, and more specifically, what families and communities can do to be an important part of the treatment process. The obvious answer to how families and communities can help people addicted to meth would probably entail support. However, the concept of support simply for the sake of supporting is actually quite risky. When it comes to meth addiction, often users become quite adept at taking advantage of other people around them, especially those who unconditionally support them with no accountability. Deception and manipulation often become paramount, and the loved one or the concerned community member showing them support often has feelings of his or her being used and perhaps even preyed upon. Take the example of Janice:

> Janice was 29 and was a master at getting what she wanted out of other people, which was that they help her to get meth, to use it, to take on her responsibilities, or help her avoid the negative consequences because of her meth use. More than once, her parents had lied to the police about her whereabouts and her

activities because she had them convinced that the police only wanted to catch her doing something wrong, since they had been paid off by her ex-husband who was trying to frame her and get sole custody of their children. She had also convinced the pastor from her church to give her housing assistance in the form of cash as opposed to a check made out to the landlord, by saying that her landlord was an immigrant and did not have a way of cashing a check. She was eventually evicted out of her apartment for nonpayment of rent. She used the money she had received from the pastor to buy drugs.

The principles and strategies discussed in this book are for community and family members to become productively involved in the treatment process of those addicted to meth. They go far beyond the simple idea of support and are designed to provide a systematic way to think about meth addiction; to consider the change needed if they are going to stop; and most important of all, to be actively involved in the treatment with other people and agencies from the community to help bring about the most promising outcome centered on recovery and long-term sobriety.

A brief discussion regarding the effect that meth has on users' relationships with their sober community is warranted at this point. While addiction to meth may develop quickly, especially when compared to other substances of abuse, the alienation of meth users from their sober communities is not something that develops simply overnight. Often people who start using meth are not, or were not, always the most stellar members of the community. In most communities, people addicted to meth tend to be poor Caucasian adults who have worked primarily in blue-collar jobs. They may have had addiction problems before meth use, including addiction to alcohol. Before using meth, they may have already developed legal problems, such as underage drinking or being a minor in possession of marijuana. As was previously mentioned, meth not only creates almost orgasmic sensations of pleasure but also fabricates a community of close users who are often enmeshed. Needless to say, then, that people who are addicted to meth are a tight-knit community. Many in their community were never very meaningfully integrated into their sober community because of their own attitudes, actions, and choices.

From the sober community, many people see very little reason to try to rehabilitate meth-using people let alone try to integrate them into a community that they may have already rejected. Furthermore, since becoming meth addicts, individuals have unlikely been law abiding and more likely been lying, manipulating, stealing, and basically taking advantage of anyone in their path to get meth, use it, and not get caught. Their crimes and misdeeds certainly have not been without negative effects on many innocent people. Users selfishly put their addiction above all else in their life. From this perspective, it seems obvious that the best treatment approach for people addicted to meth is long-term incarceration.

The lay understanding of meth addiction is primarily through the media. This understanding is that once people are addicted to meth, they can never stop using it and very few of them are ever able to get into treatment. Even those who do go to treatment are so severely changed that treatment seldom works. So it would appear that there is a population of people addicted to meth, who are likely to continue in their path of addiction with all of the antisocial and criminal acts that go along with it. There is little that can be done to help them.

The idea that treatment for meth addiction is not possible is really incorrect. Although research does support that it may take more than one treatment attempt before individuals are able to be successful. Nonetheless, if the general opinion is that people addicted to meth are drug-using and criminally minded monsters who prey on innocent members of their community, then the idea that this book proposes, that treatment should be community based, is quite hopeless. It is hopeless because the sober community would just as soon have the meth-using people be gone permanently. In some communities, this approach is known as "greyhound therapy" or "geographical therapy," which means that in some cases the best approach is to try everything to help meth-using individuals to decide, that they need to leave the community and never return. This can be done by convincing them to relocate, sending them away involuntarily, such as incarceration, or simply by buying them a one-way bus ticket so that they just keep moving through town without stopping or staying in the community. For example,

> Jack worked as an on-call mental health technician employed by the local community mental health center. His responsibility was to respond to mental health emergencies involving members of his community as well as people who may just be visiting or passing through the community. The town where Jack lived was right off of a major freeway and many transient people, who were "just passing through," would often stop in the town if they had run out of resources. A big reason why many transient people would stay was that the town had the unfortunate reputation of being an easy place to get meth. This meant that Jack was often called to respond to what appeared to be mental health emergencies involving transient visitors who seemed to be in acute states of psychiatric illnesses. Many times Jack would find out that the person did not have a serious mental illness but was under the influence of meth. Unable to arrange for psychiatric care to be provided to people under the influence of drugs, Jack's only option was to hope that they would just "move on down the line." That meant that sometimes, once a meth-using patient was determined not to be a risk to self or others, Jack helped them purchase a bus ticket to travel to whatever destination the person may have described for themselves.

Before visiting whether these options work, it would be helpful to consider if members of a community would feel different if a meth-using person was a member of their family. Most likely if that were the case, then the sober family members may be tired of the using and abuse they have had to put up with because of their loved one's addiction to meth. They may even be at a point that they are ready to give up entirely on their loved one and to wash their hands completely of them and their addiction. However, it is more likely that while the family members may still be very tired of the addiction and the things their loved one does while addicted to meth, they are not ever entirely ready to wash their hands completely of their loved one, especially if there is a small glimmer of hope.

In some cases, the family, including members of the extended family of the addicted person, may have been meth users, alcoholics, or other drug users themselves. Chronic meth use has become a part of mainstream American culture, especially in rural midwestern and western communities. There are many cases of transgenerational meth use, meaning that the addiction to meth is something that is handed down, parent to child. In chapter 2, this was the case of Sasha's best friend and fellow meth user, Kimberly. Kimberly's name has been changed, but her story is the actual experience of a young woman who started to use meth because her mother and all of her mother's friends were meth addicts.

> Kimberly was the oldest of four children and was essentially burdened with entire responsibility of raising her younger siblings alone from the time she was about eight years old. It started off as simply an unwritten expectation that part of Kimberly's responsibilities in her home were to watch after her younger brother and sisters. This was especially during the time that her mom was either sleeping or using meth in a back bedroom of their small trailer/mobile home, or completely gone from the residence for days at a time. Later, it became a direct mandate from her mother that Kimberly was to take care of the children. Her mother made it clear that if her siblings were found misbehaving, then the siblings and Kimberly were punished. Kimberly's punishment was often more severe, since it was expected that she should have prevented the incident from occurring in the first place. After all, she was the oldest and the one her mother had made responsible for the care of the other children. Her punishment was always abusive, mostly verbal, although frequently physical as well.
>
> At the age of 13, Kimberly started using meth. She was introduced to it by a male "friend" of her mother's who actually was a small-time dealer. It was never established whether or not Kimberly's mother had traded meth for her permission for this 18-year-old man to rape Kimberly. Nonetheless, that is what had happened, from Kimberly's account of things. After forced sex with the young man became more frequent, Kimberly learned that if she agreed to use meth

with him before having sex, it made the experience not only more tolerable but even, occasionally, somewhat enjoyable. However, what Kimberly noticed more was that when she would use meth with him, after having sex and he would leave, she would have what seemed to be almost unlimited energy. She could use this energy to clean up the house, take care of her younger brother and sisters and then be able to go to school and pretend to her friends that she came from a functional and non-drug-using home. Her mother was always very pleased with Kimberly after she used meth, because of the chores Kim was able to get done around their home and because her mother was usually given a fresh supply of meth from the young man who was having sex with Kimberly. Inappropriate as it may sound, her mother's approval was all that really mattered to Kimberly. When she got it, she felt like she was on top of the world. So, Kimberly's addiction to meth, starting when she was 13 years old, was interwoven with so many of her core psychological processes, including pleasure gaining, energy maintaining, and approval seeking.

At age 15, Kimberly was already a full-fledged meth addict who was quickly becoming less and less concerned about the care of her younger siblings and angry with her mother. She had also become more interested in Sasha and her other friends, including much older men, with whom she would use meth.

In Kimberly's case, it really was not safe to assume that there was a sober home that she had actively rejected to seek after meth and the meth-using community. In fact, it was Kimberly's home and her mother's addiction to meth that was primarily responsible for her addiction. The "loved ones" who really cared about Kim and the possibility of her getting off of meth and getting meaningfully integrated into a sober community were not her immediate family members. With the possible exception of an out-of-state aunt whom she barely knew, there really was not anyone from Kimberly's family who could be considered a healthy representative of a sober community with which she could become meaningfully integrated. Instead, the sober community that worked with her was made up of the many child welfare workers, foster parents, treatment providers, teachers, law enforcement officers, school counselors, and others who knew about her situation at home and the bad decisions she was making. Because she had been so responsible in caring for her younger siblings for so long, many of these people knew her, liked her, and saw her use of meth as an anomaly in her character and as something they were invested in helping her discontinue.

THE FIRST STEP

The first step to be taken in community-based treatment of meth addiction is the most difficult step to take. It is believing that, in the long run, the best place for people addicted to meth to be meaningfully integrated in is within their home, in the sober community. "Sober community" does not mean exclusively the 12-step programs offered in the community. "Sober community" refers to those people close to the individuals, either because they live within the same defined geographic area or because they have some kind of a meaningful connection to them (i.e., friends or family). These loved ones have learned how to enjoy and value every aspect of their life experiences (including difficult times) without abusing or becoming dependent on any chemical substance.

Community integration of people addicted to meth is no small task. Many members from the community are against the idea. They wonder why they should assume that individuals who are addicted to meth are going to want to change their community associations in the first place. Difficult as it may seem, however, it is what must occur for several reasons. The first reason has to do with the fact that alienation from a sober community is one of the reasons meth addiction and substance abuse initially occur. Without that connection, there is no modeling, no training about how people live sober lifestyles. For example, without being integrated into some kind of a sober community, how do those addicted to meth learn how to celebrate, relax, settle down, or enjoy being with friends without using some kind of mood-altering substance? Integration with a sober community is also important because no matter what kind of treatment individuals addicted to meth may have received, if they cannot meaningfully join a sober community, then whatever benefit they may have gleaned from their treatment will be lost, and they will relapse.

This is one of many reasons why incarceration does not work as a treatment option for meth users. Incarceration does not do anything to help people learn to live sober lifestyles. All it teaches is that if they get caught there are negative consequences that can occur because of their meth use. The strong lesson learned from incarceration is not that using meth leads to negative consequences but, instead, that meth can lead to negative consequences only if you get caught. So the lesson learned is not to stop using meth but to keep using meth and just make sure not to get caught.

Often, what is taught in jail by other incarcerated peers are more ways to not get caught, as opposed to how to change the behaviors that led to incarceration in the first place. This is because too many inmates in prisons and jails are not psychologically ready to admit wrongdoing, culpability, or poor judgment in relation to their offences. It is easier, more convenient, and less damaging to self-esteem for them to continue to deny the problems that led to incarceration than it is to accept responsibility and prepare to make changes to keep it from happening again.

Even if the media hype regarding the extreme difficulty of stopping meth use once people have started is not entirely true, to sober family members and friends, the prospects of effectively helping people to stop using the drug often appear very bleak and almost hopeless. This is because they have likely witnessed many empty promises and failed attempts to stop using. They have also probably experienced what it is like to be pitted against the meth-using community, vying for the sobriety of someone who is involved in meth use. As powerful as their pleas and interventions may be, they are no match for the pull of the meth-using community.

Meth addiction is a community problem that requires community-based solutions. This is due to many reasons, including the fact that people who use meth seldom do it alone. A distinguishing characteristic of meth addiction is that people who use often do so as part of an insidious network of other users. Their involvement with other people who also use the drug is just as powerful and difficult to break as even the addiction to the drug itself. Sasha's parents became painfully aware of this as they saw her addiction to meth correlate with and exacerbate her associations with the sordid subculture of meth addicts in their community. One person, say, a caring family member or an invested professional, working with an individual against the overwhelming tide of the meth-using community, will likely be unsuccessful. The principles that follow in this chapter are to help guide true community-based efforts to address meth addiction.

COMMUNITY DEFINED

It is important to note that the term "community" is being used in its broadest sense. A community can be friends, professionals, family, neighbors, employers, and caring individuals. The definition of a community that is being used in this book is "a social group of any size with a shared purpose and investment in a common good." Communities are started by connection, which can be geographical, such as when two people live next door to one another. Connection also can be relational, such as when people are meaningfully connected because they belong to the same family or because they are coworkers. The community can be as broad as an entire town, city, or county. It also can be as narrow as the dyad relationship between siblings. Inclusion in the meth community is really determined by two simple criteria: shared use of meth and agreement not to tell anybody about it. That is it. All other connections within meth-using circles are really appendages to these two shared criteria (values). For example, take the story of Robbie:

Robbie became a meth addict so quickly it was a shock to his family and other people who knew him. During high school, he had always been a quiet young man who was more interested in playing online fantasy role-playing games than he was in doing his school work. He was smart enough to at least pass his classes, and he graduated from high school as something of a cipher. Robbie started working at a late night fast-food restaurant after high school, and there he met the first girl to ever show much interest in him. She seemed energetic and fun and not at all shy and awkward like Robbie felt most of the time. His first sexual experience happened with her late one night after the restaurant had closed, and that was when he was also first introduced to meth. Robbie was more than willing to use meth with his new girlfriend and her meth-using friends. This is because not only did it take him out of a shell he felt had held him trapped for most of his life, but it also gave him instant friends. All he had to do to keep his newfound friends was not tell anybody what they were doing.

WHAT IS EFFECTIVE TREATMENT?

Effective treatment is not just an important part of interventions attempted by community members for people they know, such as family members or friends. Effective treatment is also critically important to general community responses to the issues of meth abuse because it lies directly at the foundation of these efforts. Effective treatment means treatment that works, creates, or helps addicted people produce actual, lasting changes in their drug-using behaviors. Perhaps the only thing more important to community responses to meth than effective treatment for meth addiction is prevention. Prevention, or keeping people from trying meth in the first place, is critical in turning the tide of increasing numbers of people addicted to meth. However, unless starting out new before a problem has grown into anything significant, prevention does very little about existing cases. To handle those currently addicted to meth, communities must have effective treatment. If effective treatment is not in place, then it becomes very difficult for people to maintain momentum and avoid feelings of hopelessness when they see people they care about continue to use meth. For these reasons, effective treatment must be at the foundation of community responses to meth addiction.

The issue becomes how to distinguish effective and less effective treatment approaches. These distinctions are made through outcome research. For a particular model to be researched, the model under investigation must be rigidly specific; otherwise, it cannot be concluded that the exact model has affected the change. For research, treatment models to be investigated need to have very specific programmatic guidelines, which are often manualized. Difficulties arise, however, in the application of these very specific models into "real community" settings. Staff limitations, service restrictions, and funding often prevent the "full" implementation of these evidence-based treatment models. This situation introduces the concept of fidelity. Programs that cannot apply the model in full, and only partially implement it, are awarded various levels of fidelity based on their exact use of the model. The problem with this is that there is no evidence supporting the partial use of the model. Therefore, evidence-based models that have been proved effective are seldom implemented in full fidelity. Instead, programs relying on partial models that have no evidence supporting their use are implemented.

The solution to this situation begins at the level of program development. Rather than designing and then researching very specific programmatic guidelines, program staff can carefully define and develop parameters for effective treatment. They can test those parameters. Program staff can research parameters with the same degree of scrutiny as a specific program. Then, they can assure communities at implementation that all of the evidence supporting the parameters applies to their specific, individualized community response to meth addiction. They can make this assurance as long as the community designs a response within the parameters. The following are descriptions of these parameters.

PARAMETERS FOR TREATMENT

It is best to begin a discussion on effective community-based treatment of meth addiction by identifying the goal we are trying to accomplish. The goal is long-term sobriety, which can be defined quite simply as (1) abstaining from meth use and (2) maintaining a lifestyle and behavior that support continued abstinence from meth and all other substances of abuse. Given the unique aspects of meth addiction, there are some things that have to change in meth-using individuals' lives for them to discontinue using the drug and maintain long-term sobriety. From the discussion in chapter 3 regarding the unique aspects of meth addiction, it should be obvious that addicted individuals need to change some important aspects of their lives. If they do not change these, they are unlikely to stop using the drug and will have difficulty maintaining their sobriety. The required changes are as follows:

1. *Stabilize their pattern of sleeping and eating.*
    Poor eating and sleeping habits are characteristic of a meth-using lifestyle. Therefore, those who have the habit of using meth to control appetite or to stay awake for extended periods of time will always be

faced with the risk of relapse unless they begin to eat healthy meals on a regular basis and sleep at least seven hours every night. Just as important is the fact that extended meth use is neurotoxic. People who are recovering from meth use are essentially in need of a form of cognitive rehabilitation. Basically, what this means is that they are trying to heal an injured brain, so to speak. As would be expected in any hospital-based physical rehabilitation effort, adequate rest and nutrition are critical to the healing process. Therefore, unless addicted individuals are helped to stabilize their eating and sleeping habits, they are not only at risk of relapse but also unlikely to fully recuperate possible cognitive deficits resulting from their meth use.

2. *Stop hanging around other people who use meth.*

As previously discussed, the social forces at work not only bringing people into initial use of meth but also sustaining that use are perhaps some of the most unique characteristics of meth addiction. Social forces are some of the most powerful reasons for not only widespread meth abuse but also failed efforts of individuals to discontinue their use of the drug. Because of the way meth disrupts daily living patterns in terms of sleep and night versus day activities, using individuals almost automatically experience changes in social groups. People who are using meth are often awake for days at a time and quite active and involved in social activities. When they finally do crash, that crash may last days at a time. This change in daily living patterns often makes it quite difficult for them to maintain steady employment or other stable lifestyle patterns. Thus, meth users are distanced from potential support from other sober people, such as coworkers, when engaged in non-meth-using daily activities.

In addition to becoming distant from sober social support groups, using individuals also become closer to other meth users simply because they are awake in the middle of the night, excited, and typically anxious to be around other like individuals. This means that they seek out other people who are also using meth. Because of the heightened suspiciousness and paranoia associated with meth use, other people who use the drug tend to be intolerant of casual users simply because they do not know who they are or how they might hurt them. The old adage, "Keep your friends close and your enemies closer," is especially applicable to paranoid heavy meth users. They have a desire to maintain close contact with people who have just initiated use of the drug and started to associate with the meth-using community. Finally, from a sheer exposure standpoint, people who are abusing meth are around other meth users and involved in the meth-using community more hours simply because they do not sleep as much.

3. *Have a sober social support group that will accept them.*

Many people who are abusing meth report that they started using the drug because they developed an association with other meth users out of a need for social support. Even before they started using meth, people who tend to use often report having felt like they never really fit in with their sober community in the first place. A statement from a young woman in rural Colorado regarding why she started using meth certainly illustrates this point.

Rita was 26 years old and heavily involved in meth use and with other people who also use it. She stated, "When I first moved to town [as a teenager] it was like no one liked me or wanted to be my friend. I mean, I wasn't a home-coming queen and I wasn't no rancher's daughter that everyone knew, so people just didn't want to have anything to do with me except for the potheads and the drug addicts. As long as I would use with them, they would always be my friends."

The need for a sober social support group that will welcome an addicted individual in early stages of recovery is essential, and the importance of that need cannot be overstated.

4. *Learn to feel pleasure without using meth or other drugs.*

It has been said that meth hijacks the pleasure centers of the brain. To an extent, this is true in that users are classically conditioned to associate feeling pleasure with use of the drug to the point that pleasure becomes almost exclusively associated with the drug. This conditioning can become so strong that it becomes almost as if users cannot feel pleasure without using the drug. For users, pleasure becomes a conditioned response to having used, and using individuals literally lose the ability to associate feeling good with things that would naturally make them feel good.

5. *Generally speaking, for someone to stop using meth, they also need to get to the point that they can handle bad feelings without abusing drugs.*

Meth is so powerfully addictive because, in addition to "turning on" a sense of euphoria and pleasurable feelings, meth also "turns off" bad feelings such as cravings, depression, low self-esteem, and even more powerfully, self-disgust, despair, and self-disdain. Because meth is so effective at relieving these unpleasant feelings and replacing them with a euphoric sense of competency, attractiveness, and control, there is a double addicting effect or a double allure to using. False and inaccurate as these feelings may be, they are nonetheless powerfully reinforcing, especially, as they replace the negative and unpleasant emotional states that become more and more pronounced; and more obviously as users' lives become more disorganized, irresponsible, and less connected with experiences that could naturally provide earned feelings of self-acceptance and self-confidence.

So, for individuals who have been abusing meth for some time to be able to stop, it is imperative that they develop skills to adequately deal with negative feelings without the use of not only meth but any addictive chemical or behavior. As addicted people become better able to use these skills, their self-confidence builds on a foundation of actual accomplishments from having handled difficult situations well.

6. *For people who have been abusing meth to be able to stop, it is also critical that they change some of their automatic expectations about the drug.*

For meth users, expectations regarding the drug can become so tremendously influential that they dictate whether or not they continue to use it in spite of the negative consequences they might have experienced. Expectations, false as they may be regarding what meth will do, how it will make them feel, how it will help them solve their problems, and/or how it will help them to connect to other people, all become very automatic. It is those expectations that drive ongoing use regardless of whether or not the drug even provides these experiences for people. If they expect it to, then they will continue using. Therefore, it is easy to imagine that individuals who abuse meth will continue until they have different expectations about the drug; not only what it has done to their life, and what will happen to them if they continue to use it, but also how it effects them in the short term.

7. *For someone to be able to stop using meth, it is also imperative that they develop positive expectations regarding the likelihood of sobriety.*

If addicted individuals believe that they are not capable of stopping their meth use or if they believe some of the false information from the media regarding their chances of long-term recovery, then it is unlikely that they will stop using it. Therefore, just as important as changing expectations of the drug is the need for users to change their expectations about sobriety.

8. *Finally, and perhaps most important, it is difficult to imagine that individuals will stop using meth unless they find some kind of a spiritual meaning or purpose to their lives.*

For users, meth addiction is certainly a meaningless experience. Those who become deeply involved in the meth-using culture become very engrossed in the use of the drug and in their associations with other users. They almost completely lose a sense of any deeper meaning to their identity, purpose in life, and sense of spirituality. Therefore, it is difficult to imagine how individuals who have been abusing meth will be able to stop unless an avenue becomes available for them to find a greater meaning or purpose to their life than whatever led them to abuse meth.

These stated assumptions regarding those things that need to change for individuals to stop using meth form the theoretical base for this particular community-based approach to treating meth addiction. Practical as the eight points stated above may appear to be, they are certainly very difficult for the most treatment-motivated users to accomplish. They require the participation of many different individuals and community agencies. Some of the social changes needed that were mentioned in the previous paragraphs, such as the development of a sober social support group and changes in the meth users' peer associations, cannot occur without many different community representatives working together in behalf of meth-addicted individuals.

Given that it is difficult to imagine people who have been abusing meth will be able to stop unless they make the eight changes stated above, these points formulate the core expectations for effective treatment of meth addiction. In other words, high-quality treatment would be that treatment that has within its design the accomplishment of these objectives. The context of the treatment model would clearly state exactly how this is going to occur. Unfortunately, this is not always the case. Instead, treatment is often a duration experience in which individuals are exposed to other sober individuals and ideas associated with a sober lifestyle. The hope is that they will eventually begin adopting some of those changes themselves. With meth addiction, however, the approach must be much more prescriptive and focused on the key areas needing change.

Judge Richard Samuelson is very frustrated with several people in his court who are addicted to meth. One woman in particular is about to have her parental rights terminated for her two young children because she has not complied with the court-ordered treatment plan. She did comply with completing a three-month drug treatment program, but Judge Samuelson was not able to get any information from the program about how well she did while in the program. Essentially, all he knows is that she stayed in the program for the required three months to complete the program, but as near he can tell she did not get anything out of it because the day she left the program she moved right back in with a meth-using boyfriend. She started using with him within a week.

THEORY AND PRACTICE

The community intervention model described in this book is designed to accomplish the eight treatment goals previously described. These expectations of needed changes for successful treatment can be appropriately grouped into the biological, psychological, and social domains. In the biological domain, for treatment to be successful meth-using individuals must establish regular sleep patterns. They also must begin to eat healthy and become more active. In the psychological domain, it is expected that for effective treatment, they must change their expectations about meth and sobriety. They must also learn to feel natural pleasure and to cope without using meth. Finally, in the social domain, for users to discontinue, they need to stop hanging around with other people who use meth. Instead, they must develop and spend time with a sober social support group. It also could be argued that there should be a fourth domain. The fourth domain is that individuals who are successful at stopping meth use have found spiritual purposes to their lives.

The exercises designed to target the changes in these domains are what constitute treatment. All too often, these changes are painful and difficult to make. They can be overly taxing for people addicted to meth to accomplish, which can account for the number of treatment failures associated with meth addiction. In addition, some of the changes needing to be made target conditioned responses that often become almost reflexive and therefore are things over which addicted individuals may not necessarily have complete conscious control. Because of the difficulties involved with breaking some of the associations and conditioned responses with meth and with changing ingrained using behaviors, people addicted to meth need structure and accountability to help them follow through with needed changes. Even very motivated clients who recognize that their addiction to meth is hurting them need more than just their own motivation to be successful in treatment. Structure and accountability provide the necessary environment for the important steps of treatment to take place.

The metaphor of sharpening an axe may be helpful in understanding how effective treatment for addiction to meth takes place (see figure 4.1). Just as a sharpening stone is needed to sharpen an axe, certain change strategies, in the form of treatment, are needed to help people break their meth addictions. These strategies include stabilizing eating and sleeping patterns, distancing from meth-using people, and meaningfully integrating with a sober community. It is important for the user to change expectations about meth and sobriety, and break the association of meth and pleasure. They must also learn to feel pleasure naturally, learn to handle difficult feelings and situations without meth or other drugs, and connect with something spiritual. These change

Figure 4.1
Meth Treatment Compared to Sharpening an Axe

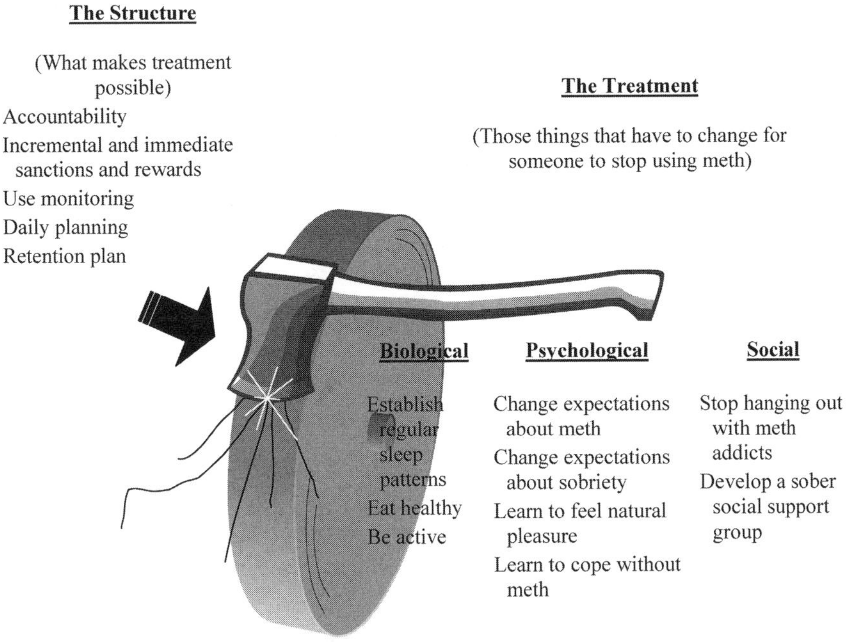

<u>**The Structure**</u>

(What makes treatment
possible)

Accountability

Incremental and immediate
  sanctions and rewards

Use monitoring

Daily planning

Retention plan

<u>**The Treatment**</u>

(Those things that have to change for
someone to stop using meth)

<u>Biological</u>	<u>Psychological</u>	<u>Social</u>
Establish regular sleep patterns	Change expectations about meth	Stop hanging out with meth addicts
Eat healthy	Change expectations about sobriety	Develop a sober social support group
Be active	Learn to feel natural pleasure	
	Learn to cope without meth	

Source: Dr. Nicolas Taylor, 2008.

experiences are difficult for people addicted to meth, as they require some-times painful and uncomfortable adaptations. In the same way that an axe will not be sharpened unless there is pressure holding it against a spinning sharp-ening stone, people addicted to meth have difficulty accomplishing the needed change strategies unless they have some kind of pressure keeping them engaged in treatment. They need pressure and structure beyond simply attending treatment sessions but more importantly, so that they do the treat-ment exercises designed to help them make the needed changes. Treatment cannot occur without the structure, just like an axe could not be sharpened without pressure keeping it against a sharpening stone.

Furthermore, pressure in and of itself is not a solution. Just as a sharpening stone is required to sharpen the axe, actual treatment of those contributing factors of meth use are required for treatment to work. Simply structuring or pressuring individuals to not use meth does not adequately address the reasons why they use. It does not ensure that needed treatment is actually provided. Therefore, effective community-based treatment for meth addiction really is a well-orchestrated combination of these two elements. Element one is the structure that is required to keep individuals in treatment and to keep them focused so that they can maximally benefit from it. The second element is effective treatment, which is supported by structure and accountability to help accomplish the needed changes in the biological, psychological, and social domains. If these changes are not made, then it is expected that addicted people will continue their meth-using lifestyles.

Before going into detail about how to create structure and exactly how community-based treatment happens in this model, it is necessary to first discuss three basic principles relevant to effective treatment for meth addiction. The first principle is the critical nature of case management. Second is the focus on outpatient success, and the third principle is the distinction between substance abuse treatment and substance counseling.

CASE MANAGEMENT

The commitment to case management is an essential and fundamental principle of this treatment model. Case management is all about helping individuals who are trying to stop using meth to be able to meet their basic needs. These needs can be things like having a safe place to live, keeping loved ones protected, employment, child care, food, and clothing. Considered by many to be the father of humanistic psychology, psychologist Abraham Maslow proposed theory of motivation, which is based on a hierarchy of human needs. His theory holds that before people are motivated to take care of what he calls "higher needs," things like gaining the respect of other people or having a high self-esteem, they are first motivated to take care of basic physiological needs. These basic physiological needs include eating and sleeping, as well as safety needs such as their security, housing, employment, and good health (see figure 4.2). Maslow's hierarchy of needs applies directly to the foundational principle of case management in the treatment of meth addiction because people receiving are not going to be motivated to benefit from treatment unless they have a way of meeting their basic needs.

Case management in this treatment approach is not about other people or agencies assuming the primary responsibility of providing for the basic needs of people who are in treatment for meth addiction. Rather, it is expected that people in treatment can and should take care of their own needs and the needs of those who depend on them. However, even when very motivated to care for themselves, many people addicted to meth lack some of the most basic skills and abilities required to do this successfully. They may not have been adequately

Figure 4.2
Maslow's Hierarchy of Needs

Source: Adapted from Abraham Maslow, "A Theory of Human Motivation," *Psychological Review* 50 (1943): 370–96.

socialized to provide for themselves. In addition, their ability to care of themselves may have been compromised by the effects of their meth use. These effects can be psychological, such as cognitive processing deficits associated with the neurotoxicity of meth. They also can be social, such as when individuals in romantic relationships develop unhealthy dependencies on other partners.

Case management is at the foundation of quality meth treatment because people in treatment have to be motivated and provided with the needed training, resources, and opportunities to be able to take care of themselves. At no point should the treatment community assume full and never-ending care for people's basic needs except in cases of severe disability, such as that faced by developmentally disabled or physically disabled individuals. Case on point, society expects people with serious mental illnesses to assume as much of the responsibility for their own care as possible to avoid unhealthy dependencies.

People recovering from addiction who are unable to meet their basic needs because of impairments that may have resulted from their meth use should be expected to do the same.

The situation with meth addiction may be seen by some to be an exception. People who were healthy before their use chose to bring upon themselves the disability because of the bad choices they made to continue meth use over a long period of time. However, it is really no different from individuals whose disability came about because they chose to drink and drive and were subsequently in an alcohol-related accident or a young person who made the bad choice to dive into a lake without knowing how deep it was. In these cases, bad choices resulted in injury that created disabilities. Blaming the persons for their bad choices does little to help with the immediate need at hand, which is to help them to become as self-sufficient as possible.

Case management with people disabled by their meth use should be no different. As with any traumatic brain injury, neurological damage caused by meth use is irreversible. It is impossible to predict how capable any person will be at adapting to the changes in their cognitive abilities to still keep functioning well and be able to handle daily life demands. It makes sense to borrow from the cognitive rehabilitation discipline as one considers effective treatment interventions for meth addiction. Cognitive rehabilitation therapists are quite capable of identifying not only specific areas of deficit that may occur because of particular brain trauma but also capabilities their patients still have and exercises they can do to improve their abilities. At the top of the list of important abilities are those required for basic self-care.

Not only is it important that communities and helping individuals do not entirely assume the case management responsibilities, which may create an unhealthy dependency on the part of the meth addict in treatment. It is also important that case management support treatment by every agency and helping individual involved in the person's care. Case management services are simply too big, complex, and difficult for one person or agency to manage. The most effective case management services are those that connect individuals with resources they require to meet their case management needs themselves, rather than one agency (or one person) simply taking care of them all by itself.

When Rod first came into treatment he was homeless and unemployed. Interestingly enough, he bragged during his intake session about the amount of money he was able to make selling meth. However, he also admitted that he never used any of that money to take care of himself or his needs. Instead, he would simply use it to buy more meth to sell and to support his own heavy use.

A local employer who had difficulty keeping job positions filled had been contacted by the community meth task force. At first the employer balked at the idea of having people who had been addicted to meth work for him because he blamed drug and alcohol abuse as the main reason he was not able to keep help in the first place. However, when he heard about Rod's accountability to a drug court judge and the drug testing he was undergoing he was willing to give him a chance. Rod ended up loving his job and becoming a valued employee. With the steady income he started receiving, he was able to pay his share of the rent of a small apartment he shared with a coworker.

Case management represents the first and most foundational aspect of community-based treatment. Communities comfortable enough to work as a team to come up with resources, ideas, and strategies that might be needed to help people in treatment meet their own needs lay the ground work upon which effective treatment can be delivered. It is unwise to have just one person assume all of the duties of meeting the basic needs of people in treatment. Furthermore, the demands for services and resources will be more than one person can provide or arrange to be provided even for just a few people in treatment. The level of dysfunction and the chaotic lifestyle associated with meth abuse simply create more needs than can be reasonably addressed by just one person or even by just one agency. For this reason, the first true test of community-based treatment is the degree to which communities are able to share the burden of case management needs for people addicted to meth who are in treatment. Communities may have one person or one agency primarily responsible for overseeing case management the services to be provided. However, the plan to make services happen should be shared by the entire community.

The following are some examples of various case management needs and creative ways communities can work together to provide for those needs:

Case Management Need
Housing (Immediate Need)
Case Scenario
Stephanie was observed by her treatment provider being dropped off for a session by a meth-using ex-boyfriend whom she had agreed to stay away from. When she was asked why she was with him, she became angry and explained that she needed a place to stay because she had gotten in a fight with her mother with whom she was living and her mom kicked her out of the house.
Creative Community-Based Solution
The treatment provider first puts the burden on Stephanie to find out where else she can go to live, even for just a short time. Wherever she decides to live must be a sober environment and safe for her and any

dependents she may have. If Stephanie continues to insist that she has no place else to go, then to show her that the community is serious about helping her to stop using meth by getting away from other people who use it, the treatment provider immediately calls the case management specialist for assistance. The case management specialist offers a donated voucher to stay at a local hotel for one night.

In addition, the case management specialist provides the names and phone numbers of several people from the community who had previously volunteered to stay the night at a hotel to keep an eye on someone if ever needed. This person, or couple, agrees to stay in the adjoining room next to Stephanie's and to simply make sure she stays there through the night. They may tie a string to her room door or ask the night clerk to let them know if she ever leaves.

The next day Stephanie meets with the case management specialists and others as needed to plan a more long-term solution to her housing crisis. This may involve her meeting with her mother and a third party to see if they can resolve their differences or it may mean that she moves into program-sponsored housing (see next item).

Case Management Need
Housing (Long-Term Need)
Case Scenario
"Hooter" was 19 years old and just released from having served 90 days in a county jail for possession of meth. Prior to going to jail he lived with his older brother, "Tooter," who was on parole for distribution of meth. While not yet violated, it was obvious to most community leaders that Tooter was selling again and that if Hooter moved back into the apartment they were sharing together after his release from jail, he would go right back to using. Hooter was eligible for drug court, but a big obstacle in his outpatient treatment was that he was not able to stay away from people who use meth. This was especially true for Hooter since his brother and all of his friends were so involved in the meth-using community.
Creative Community-Based Solution
As with many drug court participants, Hooter needs a different housing arrangement so he can stay away from the meth-using culture and have a chance to let the program work in his favor. Fortunately for Hooter, members of the community meth task force anticipated this need and devised a solution. Through the local property management and realtors' association

they were able to identify a landlord for a two-unit duplex that could comfortably house eight people. This particular landlord was known in the community because while the property was suitable it was not the nicest in town and he had difficulty keeping it fully rented. In addition, he had evicted the last two tenants for nonpayment of rent, which had required considerable time and court costs. As a result, he had become quite frustrated with the property and had been trying to sell it without much success.

Because Hooter was not the only drug court participant in need of housing, members of the community meth task force were able to approach the landlord about the possibility of renting out the two units to people who were in drug court. At first he was not interested at all, especially since he was sure that the tenants he had to evict had been using drugs, but when community leaders described to him the level of accountability and structure that was required of drug court participants he became more interested.

He especially liked that the participants were expected to pay rent biweekly instead of monthly and that he would be contacted every two weeks by the drug court coordinator to make sure all participants had paid their rent. Then, once he found out that they were accountable directly to the judge to not only take care of their bills but also to follow through with treatment and to stay away from drugs and alcohol, he was more than willing to draw up lease agreements with Hooter and the other participants in the drug court. He was even willing to allow some of the participants to pay their deposit two weeks after they had moved in, since they had just started working. All eight participants were men who were committed to the program, and extra effort was made by law enforcement and other community agencies to keep close tabs on the property and the people living there.

After a year of having the agreement with the landlord things had gone well. There was some turnover in the tenants as people completed treatment and as others went back to jail, but there was always a new person identified by the drug court team who could pick up the lease so the landlord never had to worry about empty slots.

Case Management Need
Transportation
Case Scenario
After she gave birth to her infant son, Jill moved home to live with her mother and her step father, in part, to get help taking care of her son,

but also so she could get away from the baby's father who was a local heavy user of meth. Jill herself had also been heavily involved in meth use for the two years she was with this man, but then she had stopped when she became pregnant.

Jill was motivated for treatment to help her follow through with her stated intentions to stay away from meth and other people who use it, including her baby's father. A dependency and neglect case had been opened on Jill when she was pregnant and still living with the baby's father. As part of this case, she had entered a family drug court and was enrolled in intensive outpatient therapy.

Jill's main struggle with her therapy and with other things she was trying to do in her life was that she did not have a driver's license. She had a driving under the influence five years previously and then had been arrested three times for driving with a revoked license. As a result, Jill was ineligible for a driver's license for at least two more years. Her parents live several miles out of town, and she relied on them to give her rides to where she needed to be.

Her problem was that both of her parents worked and they only had one vehicle, which made getting to her treatment sessions, drug tests, and other appointments difficult for her to do. Her frustration with her situation was obvious to those working with her, and it seemed to be getting worse to the point that there was concern that she may give up on her treatment and on her involvement in the family drug court.

Creative Community-Based Solution

Those working with Jill must start by helping her to see that they are aware of her situation, her frustration with it, and her need to get something figured out. Nonetheless, they should not immediately jump to solve her problem for her but instead ask her to come up with a plan for what she thinks will work and how they might be able to help.

This was done, and Jill shared with the treatment team that she had trouble mainly getting home from her treatment sessions that met in the evenings three nights a week. This was because her stepfather worked at night and while he could drop her off for her treatment session her mother had no way of coming to town to pick her up when they were finished. She had tried to get rides from some of the other group members, but none of them were going her way, and most of them had to get rides from their support systems.

The treatment team decided to talk with Jill and her parents about her transportation situation, and when they did, they found out that things were actually worse than they thought. Jill had to be able to come to the drug testing agency twice a week for urine tests, but the days she had to come in were random, so her parents could not plan for a ride for her on those days, and the agency closed at 5:00 P.M., which meant that her mom had to try to leave early from her job to get her and to take her to the agency. Jill's mom made it known that her employer was not happy that she had been leaving early and that she had even been told that she might lose her job if she continued to miss work.

As there was no public transportation in their small rural town, the treatment team had previously spoken with the only taxicab company in town to find out information about times of operation and fares. They had learned that the owner of the cab company also owned a small self-serve car wash and that he would often park his cab, or have his driver park their cabs, so that he could get his car wash cleaned, the bays sprayed out and the products restocked.

The treatment team decided to contact the owner of the cab company to see if he would be willing to provide free cab rides for Jill coming home from her treatment sessions, three times a week, and to and from her drug tests, twice a week. In exchange for the free cab rides, Jill would agree to be taken to the car wash after her drug tests twice a week, be dropped off for a period of time, and take car of everything that needed to be done in regard to the upkeep of the car wash. Once she was finished her work would be inspected by either the cab driver or the owner, whoever it was that was going to be taking her home.

The owner responded very favorably to the prospect of not having to pull either himself or one of his drivers off the road to take care of the car wash. Jill was grateful that she no longer had to feel like she was such a burden to her parents having to get rides to and from her appointments. The cab owner ended up being quite impressed with Jill and the work she did, which laid the groundwork for possible future employment.

Case Management Need
Employment and Child Care
Case Scenario
Cheryl was an ideal candidate for the outpatient drug treatment program except for the fact that she could not afford the cost of drug testing. The rigorous accountability required by the program had her receiving two random urine tests a week as well as a monthly hair test. Cheryl has two preschool-aged children and earned only a small income from being

a part-time waitress at a local truck stop. Her biggest barrier to employment was child care because her job paid her barely enough to pay for child care, and in some cases when her hours were cut to part-time she was actually losing money.

Creative Community-Based Solution

The case manager met with Cheryl to help her troubleshoot her financial situation. The case manager discovered that the day care provider Cheryl was using insisted on charging for full days with her kids, which meant that on days when Cheryl was only working for part of the day, she still had to pay for the full day. The case manager, working with the community meth task force, was able to help Cheryl find better employment as an aid at a large preschool and day care facility run through a local church. She was able to bring her kids to work with her, and while she helped out in the preschool as a teacher's aid, her kids were able to stay in the day care. Her work in the preschool was still just part-time in the mornings, but she was able to keep working as a waitress in the afternoon and then pick her kids up from day care at the end of the day. The added income helped Cheryl be able to afford her treatment as well as her drug testing.

A good way to think about case management involves the metaphor of a hurricane. For people who are abusing meth and living deep in the meth-using culture, it is like being in the middle of a hurricane. The chaos and instability of the meth-using world take on almost hurricane-like qualities. To users, night becomes day, and day becomes night. Users find it nearly impossible to determine friend from foe and to escape both real and imagined sources of threat. Case management is about providing a pavilion of protection from the storms of chaos associated with meth addiction. Most of that chaos is created by the inability or the lack of regard to take care of basic needs, and they have few things in their lives that are stable and predictable. It can be argued that many of the symptoms of dysfunction associated with meth addiction could be just as much about the unstable lifestyle associated with using meth as they are about the effects of the drug itself. These symptoms can include but are certainly not limited to paranoia, poor health, cognitive dysfunction, and lifestyle instability. The first step in any treatment experience is to assure that case management needs are being met.

When Sarah first came in to ask for help from the public health nurse, she was a mess. She was 19 years old, four months pregnant, had no place to live, and was waiting for the man who got her pregnant to get out of jail so that they could figure out what they were going to do. She had been living with her maternal grandmother since she ran away from her parents' home in another state when she was just 17. Her grandmother was overwhelmed having to care for three young grandchildren from Sarah's aunt. Her aunt was also a meth addict who was about to have her parental rights to these children terminated.

Sarah was actually introduced to meth by her aunt, when she met her baby's father, a man who also used meth and was 10 years her senior. Her grandmother warned her about what she was doing and told her that if she "wound up pregnant," she could not count on her for support and would be no longer welcome in her home. Sarah had actually stopped using meth even before she became pregnant because she had a frightening experience while high, during which she became terrified that her romantic partner's ex-wife was trying to kill her. Even though she had stopped using meth, her lifestyle, lack of stability, and inability to meet even her basic needs made it seem as if she was still very much involved in meth use. In fact, the pubic health nurse was quite surprised when her drug test came back negative for meth.

Case management needs can be summarized in a series of questions regarding the stabilization of biological, psychological, and social needs. The questions shown in table 4.1 are designed to help evaluate whether or not a case has been adequately managed, in other words, whether or not the individual's lifestyle has been adequately stabilized for him or her to receive maximum benefit from treatment.

FOCUS ON OUTPATIENT SUCCESS

Another guiding principle is that of the need for outpatient success. A focus on making outpatient therapy as beneficial as possible is critical for effective community-based treatments of meth addiction. That is because no matter how well people may do in inpatient treatment, their treatment is not successful until they develop the ability to adequately apply those skills in an outpatient setting. So while inpatient treatment may be necessary and of some benefit, the "rubber" really does "meet the road" in outpatient treatment when clients are given opportunities to begin applying some of those skills to deal with the challenges of their lives without using meth in their day-to-day living situations.

What this means for communities and families trying to intervene with people who are addicted to meth is that the lure of getting individuals help by only sending them off to inpatient treatment to get them away from the meth-using community is misleading and an inadequate strategy to treat the problem. If people do need inpatient treatment, it is still best to have them start in outpatient programs even if it seems quite clear that they will not be

Table 4.1
Case Management Checklist

Biological	Psychological	Social
✓ Does the client have a safe place to live?	✓ Are the client's withdrawal symptoms being effectively managed?	✓ Is the client interacting effectively with many people during the daytime hours?
✓ Does the client have the ability to provide for his or her basic needs as well as those of dependent family members?	✓ Does the client have the skills to deal with cravings and to avoid relapse?	✓ Is the client living with anyone who abuses drugs or alcohol?
✓ Are the client's acute medical issues being effectively treated?	✓ Has the client been evaluated for antidepressant medication if needed?	✓ Is the client living in an environment that is safe for the individual and/or others who depend on him or her, such as children?
✓ Is the client eating three healthy meals a day?	✓ If so, is the client taking the medication as prescribed?	✓ Does the client have regular contact with supportive and sober friends, family and community members?
✓ Is the client sleeping at least six hours each night?	✓ Is the client suicidal?	✓ Is the client being threatened, or is the person under any kind of duress from other people who are still using meth?
✓ Is the client falling asleep by 11:30 P.M. and out of bed by 8:00 A.M.?	✓ Does the client have sufficient energy in the morning to get out of bed and face the day?	✓ Is the client threatening harm against any other person?
✓ Has the client improved his or her self-care and grooming habits?	✓ Is the client showing improvement in his or her cognitive functioning?	
✓ Is the client taking all physician-prescribed medications as instructed?		

successful at that level of care. Caution must be taken to not ignore serious issues of harm to self or others that may necessitate immediate admission into a controlled environment. However, even in these cases, long-term residential treatment may still not be the best and certainly not the most economical option. A controlled environment should be short-term, with the least intensive level of care necessary to help people to stabilize, so that they can be admitted back into outpatient treatment as soon as possible.

There are several reasons why there should be a focus on outpatient treatment from the beginning, even in cases in which inpatient treatment is an obvious necessity. First, individuals receiving the treatment need to see that the measure of success will be their abilities to make it in outpatient settings. They need to understand that inpatient treatment is used only as a support for the outpatient treatment, which is the main focus of every treatment experience. In addition, if individuals receiving treatment begin by establishing relationships with outpatient treatment providers, when they complete their inpatient treatment experiences, they will be more likely to feel comfortable with the inpatient-to-outpatient transition because they will be working with providers with whom they have already established trusting relationships. That transition is like passing a baton in a relay race. In many cases in which the focus is mostly on inpatient treatment with little or inadequate planning for outpatient follow up, that baton often gets dropped. Discharge planning into outpatient treatment should begin the moment individuals enter into inpatient treatment. Inpatient treatment should be kept as short as possible, so that it is used only to stabilize and prepare people to return to an outpatient treatment setting, where real changes occur.

A question is whether it is possible for outpatient treatment to be successful given the powerful social dynamics of the meth-using community and given that individuals in outpatient treatment are not as physically separated from that community as they are when they "go away" to inpatient treatment. That outpatient treatment is tremendously challenging is true, especially because individuals in treatment are at every moment confronted with the option of abandoning their treatment and allowing the powerful social forces of the meth-using community to bring them back into association with other meth-using people and to keep using the drug. However, challenging does not mean impossible. Furthermore, if the issue of the influence of the meth-using culture is so paramount to treatment success, then fleeing from it into temporary inpatient treatment does not give people opportunities to directly address what may be the biggest challenge to their sobriety. Nor does it give them the chance to confront this issue with the direct support, accountability, and supervision that can be offered by an outpatient community-based treatment model.

One of the biggest reasons community-based treatment provided in an outpatient setting is necessary and effective in treating addiction to meth is that it does provide this opportunity. In fact, if it is assumed that the need for individuals trying to stop using meth is to get away from others who still use it is so critical, then it only makes sense that treatment focus on helping address this issue from the beginning is preferable. It is preferable to simply avoiding the issue and hoping that the problem will simply resolve itself, which it seldom does.

Inpatient treatment may be a necessary first step to getting the required buffer to be able to begin with the kind of community-based outpatient treatment being talked about here. However, every effort should be made to keep the inpatient treatment from becoming the primary treatment focus. It must be short and used only as a supplement to outpatient treatment where all who are involved in the treatment experience know and understand that the goal is to stop using meth and to stay away from those who do use it. Since it is unreasonable to assume that individuals could ever live in long-term inpatient treatment, their progress in this experience and the quality of the program is measured in how well they do, not while in the inpatient setting, but later when they return home.

The strategies and sober living skills learned in inpatient treatment can be of tremendous benefit but often take on a very hypothetical feeling. People in inpatient treatment are forced to ask themselves what they might do "if" or "when" they are confronted with a particular relapse situation. They may learn some new things that will be helpful, but absent the proving grounds of day-to-day life these newly acquired skills and their intentions and plans are untested. They may work well once they return home, but they will find that it was one thing to think and plan what they might do in particular high-relapse potential situations, and it becomes quite another thing when they begin applying what they have learned. Often no amount of foresight and planning is possible to prepare people for everything they will encounter within their home environment that will challenge even the best of their intentions of staying away from meth and those who use the drug.

Outpatient treatment is very much a "learn as you go" process because addicted people have the opportunities to try out new skills and seek help refining what they need to do to stay sober on an ongoing basis. They are given opportunities to bring to their treatment sessions not hypothetical situations of what they anticipate the challenges to their sobriety to be, but rather real-life, day-to-day experiences, many of which may have just occurred or may be occurring at the moment they enter an outpatient treatment session. These immediate and true tests of treatment effectiveness are not available in inpatient treatment. Regardless of how they may have done in inpatient treatment, if they cannot apply what they have learned once they return to their home environment, then that treatment experience was not successful.

In addition to providing true testing grounds for the application of sober living skills, outpatient treatment offers something of even greater value in terms of ways to help people addicted to meth to stop using it. What outpatient treatment has to offer is the opportunity to help addicted individuals become integrated into a sober social support system within their home communities. As opposed to simply telling individuals that it is necessary for them to change who their friends and other sources of social support need to be, community-based outpatient treatment can create the vehicle through which this happens.

Treatment strategies described in this approach have several purposes, but always one of the main ones is to help addicted individuals become meaningfully connected with sober communities. For this reason, the strategies are quite prescriptive and always have as their goal that of taking sometimes reluctant users in treatment by the hand and leading them to sober lifestyles with sober and pro-social support systems. The ex-users still must allow the connections to be made, but an important strategy for the people helping with treatment is to provide individuals with meaningful niches within sober communities. An important reason why Chris in chapter 2 was able to make some of the changes he did was that he was offered sincere and genuine connections within the sober community.

TREATMENT VERSUS COUNSELING

The third basic principle of this approach is the distinction between substance abuse treatment and counseling. As was explained in chapter 3, addiction to meth is quite unique because it often involves the development of automatic associations that become almost like reflexes for addicted individuals. The association between feeling good or not feeling bad (positive and negative reinforcement) and the use of meth become so firmly ingrained because of the powerfully reinforcing properties of the drug that people almost lose the ability to feel pleasure from anything else. Feeling good and/or not feeling bad for them becomes all about using meth. Changing these kinds of conditioned associations requires more than mere advice giving. Counseling can be thought of as giving advice within the influence of a generally supportive relationship to help encourage and facilitate change. Because so much of what meth does to people's lives has to do with altering reflexes and conditioned responses, counseling individuals is only of mild benefit and does not fully address the problem.

Treatment can be thought of as the use of directed interventions designed to target specific psychological processes, which are believed to underlie people's addiction to meth. In this way, treatment is very hands-on and specific. It is as if those addicted have conditioned responses over which they have lost all control. In this way treatment of addiction to meth is quite similar to treatment of conditioned anxiety, such as can be found with people diagnosed with PTSD. People who develop PTSD do so in part because trauma, especially trauma that is perceived as life threatening, is so significant that they remember it in a way different from other experiences. They remember it not just because the traumatic event is indelibly recorded in long-term memory but because of the perceived connection between all of the cues associated with the event and their survival. They record these cues even though they have no logical connection to the traumatic event. For example, the smell of an air freshener in a car right before an accident can later trigger traumatic reactions. So can an intersection where the accident took place or even the time of day and season of the year when the accident happened. These cues, while certainly not a cause of the accident, nonetheless trigger the reexperiencing of the trauma for people suffering from PTSD. While important, and a necessary context in which treatment takes place, supportive counseling is not sufficient for the person to be able to recover completely from the trauma. They need help reprocessing and "rewiring" their memory of the event and the cues associated with it. The more the cues from the person's life that trigger the anxiety and/or the more sensitive those cues are, the more debilitated the person will be by their PTSD responses.

As has been established, meth is powerfully reinforcing. So much so that the memory of using meth can become as indelibly recorded in the mind with all the peripheral cues, as memories for trauma tend to be. Therefore, memory of the "meth high" and all of the situational cues that signal using opportunities are almost unconsciously remembered, and the presentation of all or any of the cues can cause a psychological reexperiencing of what it is like to be high. In addition, the association between meth use and the many unconditioned stimuli with which meth may have been paired (i.e., celebrating, relaxing, getting productive, etc.) can become so strong that individuals have difficulties experiencing these events without the use of meth. Their expectations of meth, even if untrue, can become automatic and almost involuntary.

It is for these reasons that treatment for meth addiction necessitates a more prescriptive and directed approach than might be used in simple substance abuse counseling. Although the positive secondary factors of counseling, such as interpersonal regard, listening, and empathy are certainly necessary as well, they are not sufficient to provide the kind of help needed by people addicted to meth. Using the metaphor of digging up a post, treatment interventions for meth addiction are needed to "get under" the addiction to meth as much as getting a shovel under a fence post is necessary to dig it out. If the digging does not go deep enough to get under the fence post to dig it out, then it is unlikely to move. If treatment does not go deep enough to address some of the automatic behaviors associated with meth addiction, then it is unlikely to be sufficient to help produce real change in the addicted person's long-term using behaviors.

As was mentioned regarding the approach to community-based treatment presented in this book, a balance is needed between treatment and structure, the things that are needed for treatment to take place. It will be recalled that earlier in this chapter treatment was compared to a sharpening wheel and structure, to the pressure applied to an implement to hold it against the wheel. The next chapter will address the issue of structure.

CHAPTER 5

Creating Structure

Effective meth treatment involves successfully helping addicted individuals make key changes in their lives. These changes include staying away from other people who use meth, developing close friendships with sober people, sleeping and eating well, being able to handle difficult situations without using, and being able to feel good without using while changing some of their automatic expectations and beliefs about meth. All of these changes are needed to accomplish the final goal of abstaining from meth altogether and living a sober lifestyle. Obviously, this is easier said than done, and helping individuals make these changes requires many people working together. As has been noted, the chances that just one person or one agency would be able to help someone who is addicted to meth make these changes are very slim. However, many people and agencies working together are much more likely to be successful.

STAGES OF CHANGE AND READINESS FOR CHANGE

These helping efforts require an organizing strategy since saying that people need to change their behavior is one thing, but helping them to do it is something entirely different. Strategies communities and families can use do rely on the addicted person's having at least some investment in making the needed changes, even if the person's investment is based on nothing more than staying out of trouble or out of jail, getting off of probation, or getting one's children back. These are the important sanctions and rewards that are part of the accountability and structure needed for treatment to work.

They help to create the right kind of environment for change, but change itself is a process. Other people cannot assume responsibility for the changes, any more than a gardener can assume the responsibility of making a plant grow.

> Enid had been trying for years to get her adult daughter Julie off of meth. She had expended almost all of her retirement savings paying for one failed inpatient treatment after another. Each time Julie would respond well while in treatment, her mother and others would become hopeful and excited, believing that she was finally ready to stop using meth and change her life. However, without fail, Julie would come home after treatment, do well for a time, and then eventually go right back to her using friends and start using meth with them. Enid wondered what it was finally going to take to get Julie to stay away from the drug. She wondered if she had the strength to get through this difficult time.

There are different stages in the change process. Prochaska, DiClemente, and Norcross (1992) studied the change process of people trying to break habits like quitting smoking, eating poorly, or not exercising. They found that change actually occurs in a series of stages. The first stage of change is not really a stage but more of a starting point, depending on the state of mind people are in, when they see no real need for change and feel that things for them are just fine and change is not needed. This stage is labeled pre-contemplation. When individuals begin to consider that change is needed, then they move from the pre-contemplation to contemplation stage. Those in the contemplation stage are still not ready to change but at least are considering that perhaps they should make a change in the specific area. The next stage in the change process is determination. In this stage, people considering change now take real steps toward making the change happen. They are done just thinking about it and are ready to start taking action. They begin making plans of how they will change and take serious steps toward making the change happen. For example, if individuals make decisions to stop smoking, they may share their decisions with loved ones and other people who they know will support them in their change effort. At this point, they move into the "action" stage, as they now make the needed change and follow through with their decisions. Sustaining the change requires ongoing effort and planning, and this stage is the "maintenance" stage. For some people that is enough and they simply continue maintaining the change they have made, and they basically exit the change process as the change becomes a permanent part of who they are. However, for most people old patterns of behavior sneak back in and they relapse into the behavior they were trying to change. The stage of relapse actually brings people around full cycle to the stages of pre-contemplation and then contemplation again. They become determined to try again to change, take action to make the change, and then work hard to maintain it.

The process of relapse is an interesting part of the stages of change, since it would appear that relapse brings individuals back to where they started with pre-contemplation. However, what is interesting is that, while they may initiate the change process again, it is not as if they are starting all over again. That is because they have learned more about their efforts to change and they have gained experience that makes them slightly more advanced in their change process compared to before when they did not even consider making a change.

Readiness to change has a lot to do with where they are in the stages of change. People who are clearly in the pre-contemplation stage need help feeling motivated to want to change, while those who are in the determination stage need help developing a plan of action so that they can translate their good intentions into actual change. Helping strategies to aid in the change process can be tailored to fit the needs of people depending on where they are in their readiness for change.

Enhancing motivation to follow through with change is perhaps one of the most challenging aspects of working with those addicted to meth. A common misconception regarding motivation is the belief that individuals will not change until they really want to. Desire for change is such a difficult concept to clearly identify. This is because even for highly motivated people, there is always ambivalence about whether or not they *really* want to change and whether they think they are capable of change. So, waiting until they are at an acceptable point of desiring change is unwise because that milestone of readiness may be elusive. Even if it appears that they are finally at the point when they seem like they want to change, that point could easily diminish or change simply because of their ambivalence.

What is certain is that people who use meth experience negative consequences because of their use. Even people who are in the early stages of their addiction and are still enamored with the drug, its effects on them, and their tie-in with other users experience negative consequences. It may appear that they think there is nothing at all bad about what they are doing and even feel that it is causing them no problems whatsoever. The very nature of meth addiction and the behaviors that accompany it are so opposed to what is basic humanity. With the exception of perhaps only a few truly psychopathic meth addicts, there is a sense that what they are doing is not what they want for themselves. The problem is that while they may know that it is not what they want, they may not know how to stop. Too often, their statements of defiance and apparent allegiance to meth and the meth-using culture are actually signs of defense of something they do not like. However, they do not admit they do not like meth. This is because they have little or no confidence in their ability to change. This is what happens when they are wrong, and they know it. It simply is so much easier for them to not admit, than to agree that what they are doing is not really what they want for themselves. To an extent, this element of their defensiveness is at the heart of most addictions.

Ambivalence about stopping meth use can be strong even for people clearly indicating that they are willing and want to stop using. For that reason, relying only on self-motivation for change is often not sufficient to carry most people addicted to meth all the way through the change process. It may work for some people, but for most it does not. More common, those addicted to meth will experience more negative consequences than just dissonance with themselves. They may experience consequences that can include legal problems, health problems, loss of job, loss of freedom, alienation from family and/or other sober individuals, financial problems, and/or having children taken away. Even for severely addicted individuals, these negative consequences associated with their use are something they want to avoid.

Meth users' motivation to avoid negative consequences is much more sustainable. However, negative consequences often do not produce changes in behavior, mostly because they do not occur after every time people use the substance. Furthermore, the negative consequences associated with use always occur later, after the desirable effects of the drug have worn off. Therefore, addicted people's motivation to change their use so as to avoid negative consequences waxes and wanes. This is because they think negative consequences may or may not happen from their use depending on whether they get caught. Because one of the effects of meth is that it produces a false sense of competency and control, the belief that individuals can use and not get caught is only reinforced after they start using. Besides, even if people do accept that bad things will happen to them because of their use, those unwanted outcomes always happen later, again if they happen at all.

What this means for families and communities trying to help people addicted to meth is that the best and most sustainable motivation comes from negative consequences that are reliable, immediate, and certain every time they use. Their motivation is further enhanced when every step they take in the direction of sobriety, no matter how small it is, is reinforced immediately with a reward. To be interested and invested in change, people in recovery need an environment of immediate and incremental sanctions and rewards that are directly associated with their meth use.

When people are actively using meth, their ability to sustain their focus on what they really want out of life and on what their meth use is doing to them are almost nonexistent. This is because of the hyper-distractibility associated with the drug itself and also because doing so creates such a painful awareness of inadequacy, low self-esteem, and even self-disgust that the user actively avoids allowing this to happen. Because use of meth is so effective at detouring attention and burying these unwanted emotions beneath a false sense of competency and self-acceptance, individuals will often use it just to keep from having these feelings. For these reasons, waiting for those addicted to meth to reach the realization that they need to stop and that they are capable of stopping before initiating an intervention borders on being ridiculous. This is because it may not be fair to them and because it inadequately takes into account the effects of the drug and what it does to users. Furthermore, delaying an intervention only creates additional heartache and potential for significant problems that occur during this waiting period. This is unnecessary since families and communities working with people addicted to meth can begin immediately creating the structure needed so that immediate and incremental sanctions and rewards happen as quickly as possible in response to ongoing meth use as well as steps taken toward sobriety.

This is not to suggest that inner (intrinsic) motivation is not necessary for change to happen. With addiction to meth, during the early stages of the change process, it is unrealistic to expect that the addicted individuals will be capable of generating sufficient inner motivation to overcome the addictive properties of the drug. External (extrinsic) motivation generated by positive and negative consequences provides the starting point for focus on change that eventually becomes internally driven as the addicted people detoxify. The users can then take advantage of the opportunities that the structure and accountability allow them to have. They can begin to consider the possibility of living sober lifestyles. While they are using the drug, this opportunity is simply not available to them. Therefore, structure is necessary to allow inner motivation to develop to the point that changes begin to occur not just to avoid negative consequences and to gain rewards but also because using individuals have internalized the need for change. They begin to desire it for themselves independent of the immediate consequences.

ACCOUNTABILITY

The first ingredient of therapeutic structure is accountability. Accountability refers to the addicted individuals' being held responsible for their actions. It also refers to the need to focus on what individuals do or have done as opposed to what they say they do or have done. Addiction to meth thrives in a world of lies and secrecy. In some cases, the compulsion to use the drug is enhanced by the thrill of doing it and not getting caught or of not having others realize that the person is under the influence. For this reason, structure can only be effective when it is built upon strategies that hold individuals accountable. They must be held accountable to objective measures, such as confirmed contact with identified individuals or agencies, verified distancing from key people, and the results of drug-screening tests.

It is important that meth-using individuals appreciate that the purpose of the objective measures is to help strengthen not only their accountability but also their relationship of trust with other people working with them. As much as is possible, they should be helped to understand that they must be truthful about all behaviors associated with their meth use. However, it is unlikely that they, similar to just about anyone else in their situation, will always be honest. This may simply be part of their being addicted to meth, and they should not be blamed. Taking a blame-free approach to their dishonesty regarding their meth use acknowledges but does not shame individuals for something that is very much part of their addiction to meth.

GOVERNING FORCE

The most obvious question regarding accountability is, "accountable to whom?" In some situations this is an easy question to answer, as the meth-using individuals' actions may have brought them in contact with the legal system. They are then accountable to probation officers or judges regarding behaviors associated with their drug use. Their contact with a legal system is not always because of criminal behavior. For example, in some cases meth-using parents may come to the attention of child protection services because their drug use has negatively impacted their ability to adequately care for their children. They then are accountable to caseworkers or to the courts regarding their meth-using behaviors and the degree to which they are able comply with expectations to safely parent their child(ren).

A number of people addicted to meth recognize that their use is a problem and seek help trying to stop it. They may come to this realization on their own, but more commonly it is because of other people. These other people can be family members, friends, romantic partners, church leaders, counselors, attorneys, or employers. These other people became aware of the individual's drug use and other negative behaviors associated with it. They found these behaviors to be of sufficient concern to want to help the person stop using. They may or may not have shared their concern with the person using meth. Once they have shared their concerns with the meth user, their relationship unavoidably changes. This is because the meth-using person has to come to terms with what their concerns might mean. It may mean that they are concerned about the person's meth use and want him or her to simply consider that. In contrast, it might mean that they feel so powerfully about it that ending meth use becomes a strong expectation in the relationship. The question is whether the using person should then be held accountable to the other person in this relationship? This is difficult to answer since the dynamic of accountability and having one person clearly in authority over the other is something neither person may want or have expected in the relationship.

In these situations a community-based intervention can be especially beneficial. The biggest challenge will be for the other person to determine the point at which they decide that it is worth it to risk the stability of the relationship by confronting the person addicted to meth about sharing this information with other people outside the relationship. The risk they run is what they will have to do if the person refuses. In some situations, such as the relationship of a therapist or a doctor with someone who is a patient, there may be ethical and legal restraints on what information they can share and with whom. The only tool they have to force the issue, if the patient refuses, is their relationship with the individual. This also may be especially problematic for psychologists or mental health counselors who have ethical guidelines that prohibit them from refusing to continue seeing patients because they will not agree to allow the disclosure of certain information. In these cases the only option would be to focus therapy on the necessity of including other people in the treatment and then in a noncoercive way to solicit from the patient his or her endorsement of such an approach.

Whatever the relationships with addicted individuals, if they will agree to allow other people to be brought into the issue of meth use, new options for accountability are opened up. Still, the question of who to include and why they should be the one to assume the accountability dynamic is left unanswered. Who to include in the community-based intervention is an issue. Who is closest to the addicted person, exactly what their relationship may be, and what is their motivation for wanting to get involved? Obviously, people who struggle with addiction problems are not real good candidates, nor are people who take interest in addicted people only because of unresolved caretaking needs they may have. Whoever is included in the "community" that will work with the meth user should be capable of working collaboratively with others also trying to help. This is so that decisions and assessments of how to intervene are made collectively and collaboratively. This approach provides some indication of how to handle the question of accountability. Interventions are best when accountability is to a community of caring people close to the individual, as opposed just one person.

At this point, it would be helpful to discuss the role of judicial officers, probation officers, or caseworkers in community-based interventions. While in these cases, there still may be one person who is clearly charged with making decisions about compliance, accountability, and the outcome of behaviors. It works much better if these decisions are made after hearing recommendations from many others invested in the meth-addicted individual's sobriety. A trusting relationship needs to exist between the ultimate decision maker and others from the community involved in the case. It works best if all those involved can agree to jointly endorse the final decision made by the ultimate decision maker, knowing that what that person decides may not always be in line with what they or even the majority think should happen. The more the addicted individuals feel that decisions regarding the outcomes of their behaviors are being made by a group of people representing a sober community of caring individuals, the more likely they are going to trust the processes. They will come to believe the processes are exactly what are going to be needed to help them stop using meth and to change all other behaviors associated with their patterns of using.

An example of how these basic principles have been put into practice is drug court. Over the last 20 years drug courts have been developed to strategically accomplish these objectives (Huddleston 2007). The drug court judge is usually the ultimate authority regarding the administration of sanctions and rewards to addicted individuals participating in the court. However, there usually is a team of people working with the addicted individual who help to make these decisions by reporting compliance and progress as well as by making recommendations regarding what they think should be done by the judge.

According to the publication *Defining Drug Courts: The Key Components*, published by the Bureau of Justice Assistance, there are 10 key components of a drug court model. Drug courts combine intensive judicial supervision, treatment, mandatory drug testing, and escalating sanctions and rewards to help substance-abusing offenders break the cycle of addiction and the crime that often accompanies it. Drug court judges work with prosecutors, defense attorneys, probation officers, and drug treatment specialists to determine appropriate treatment for offenders, monitor their progress, and ensure the delivery of other services, like education or job skills training, to help offenders remain crime and drug free. The 10 key components that describe the basic elements of a drug court are as follows:

1. Drug courts integrate alcohol and other drug treatment services with justice system case processing.

2. Using a non-adversarial approach, prosecution and defense counsel promote public safety while protecting participants' due process rights.

3. Eligible participants are identified early and promptly placed in the drug court program.

4. Drug courts provide access to a continuum of alcohol, drug, and other related treatment and rehabilitation services.

5. Abstinence is monitored by frequent alcohol and other drug testing.

6. A coordinated strategy governs drug court responses to participants' compliance.

7. Ongoing judicial interaction with each drug court participant is essential.

8. Monitoring and evaluation measure the achievement of program goals and gauge effectiveness.

9. Continuing interdisciplinary education promotes effective drug court planning, implementation, and operations.

10. Forging partnerships among drug courts, public agencies, and community-based organizations generates local support and enhances drug court effectiveness.

IMMEDIATE AND INCREMENTAL SANCTIONS AND REWARDS

For people addicted to meth, the step between active use and full recovery is quite a stretch and for most is almost impossible to take in one leap. For this reason, it is important that their recovery process be broken down into small steps, which if successfully taken can help the using individuals eventually accomplish the goal of long-term sobriety. These small steps begin with things as simple as just showing up for scheduled appointments, eating square meals, staying home and sleeping through a night, and remembering to call in to check about drug testing. Once mastered, individuals can then begin to take larger steps toward recovery. These include extended periods of time of verified abstinence, time spent away from other people who use meth, and maintaining employment. Sanctions and rewards are used as extrinsic factors to help shape behavior toward accomplishing each step necessary for addicted people to eventually establish and then maintain sober lifestyles. Rewards can be used to reinforce those small steps or successive approximations toward the targeted outcome of long-term sobriety.

Two important principles that must be kept in mind regarding sanctions and rewards relate to timing and degree. The greater the time lag between the behavior and the reward designed to reinforce it or the sanction designed to punish the behavior, the weaker the effect will be to either increase or decrease targeted behaviors. For this reason, rewards and sanctions should occur as quickly as possible following the desired targeted behaviors. It is also important that rewards and sanctions be graduated, so that they match the behavior they address. Small steps in the right direction deserve small rewards, and larger steps should result in more substantial rewards.

> Judge Thompson, the drug court judge, was thrilled with Susannah's progress, as were the other members of her treatment team. It may not have seemed like much to outsiders not familiar with her case, but to those who knew her well and who knew how hard it was for her to take the initial steps toward abstaining from meth use, her choice to show up for four treatment sessions in a row and to have a clean urine test was a big deal. Susannah had grown accustomed to getting out of jail and then going right back in again because she failed to show up for appointments and because her drug tests suggested that she was still using meth. Judge Thompson had almost given up on her and was about to discharge her from the program when she pled for one last chance and assured everyone involved in her case that she was serious. She testified that this time she really meant to do what she knew was going to be in her best interest. The judge and others in the court room had their doubts that she would complete what she had said she was going to do. However, when the time came for her scheduled appointment, she arrived on time and seemed generally interested in engaging in treatment. She completed the intake process and then attended three consecutive treatment sessions. She had also attended a community integration assignment from the court and had met with several volunteers from the community to help repair children's books at the local library. Her urine tests showed that she had not used any drugs for about two weeks. In response to these clear steps in the right direction, Judge Thompson and the treatment team decided to reward Susannah's progress with a surprise dinner engagement at a local restaurant.
>
> Susannah was told she was being picked up to be taken to an NA meeting, but then instead she was taken to the restaurant, where, in a private dining room, her sober close friends and family were waiting for her. Susannah had always been close to her grandmother, but she had not seen her for over two years because she had distanced herself from her and because she lived in another city. The team made arrangements for her grandmother to be there as well. Everyone who attended the dinner stood and read to Susannah brief notes of encouragement they had all prepared for the occasion. The group was most surprised when Judge Thompson showed up for a brief moment during dessert. He had prepared a brief note of encouragement for Susannah, which he shared with

her as well. She seemed to glow by the end of the night, and she expressed an even stronger commitment to stay away from meth and to be successful in the program. As it turned out, this event was a significant turning point for Susannah, who ended up successfully completing the program and changing her life.

OBJECTIVE BEHAVIORAL BENCHMARKS

Traditionally, treatment progress has been measured primarily by periods of verified abstinence or by time spent in treatment. While periods of verified abstaining from meth are a good but incomplete measure of treatment progress, time spent in treatment provides little information about how beneficial the experience may have been for the user. In spite of this, treatment continues to be measured in length of stay, and people addicted to meth are commonly mandated to go to treatment for a specific period of time. The risk of approaching treatment this way is that the focus can become more about some kind of a duration expectation, as opposed to actual change. Treatment is not like baking rolls in an oven where it is expected that if someone stays in treatment for a certain span of time, it will have the desired effect.

More reasonable measures of treatment progress, like periods of verified abstinence, involve objective verification of changes in behavior that suggest that the person is changing and that treatment does appear to be working. Periods of verified stable sleep patterns can also be used as measures of treatment progress. It can safely be assumed that even if individuals addicted to meth are no longer actively using, they are setting themselves up for a relapse if they continue a pattern of irregular sleep. This is because irregular sleep and staying awake at night are basic living patterns associated with the drug-using lifestyle. In addition, regular sleep patterns are important because individuals in recovery are also trying to recuperate/rehabilitate from the neurotoxic effects of the drug. For this to occur, it only makes sense that those in recovery get adequate rest and sleep well, so that they have the maximum possibility of a full recovery from the neurotoxic effects of meth.

Similar to stabilizing sleep patterns is the need to stabilize diet and eating patterns. Meth is an appetite suppressant, and as a result, people who use meth heavily have little desire to eat and tend to only snack occasionally on foods that are high in sugar and carbohydrates. The resulting weight loss from these kinds of diets and the hyperkineticism associated with meth use actually create motivation for use, primarily in women. Another objective measure of treatment progress is the pattern of eating manifested by those in recovery for meth addiction. If individuals recovering from meth addiction are eating three healthy meals a day, then several things will occur that are supportive of long-term sobriety. The first thing that will happen is they will be breaking yet another lifestyle cue associated with their being meth addicts. For many people, using meth and not eating are almost synonymous. When they start eating right, they establish daily protection against reminders of their old lifestyle. In addition, as with sleeping regularly, eating right is an important factor for people addicted to meth to be able to fully recover from the neurotoxic effects of their use. To regain their full cognitive functioning, they need to be eating the necessary nutrients for the brain to recuperate following the cessation of meth use.

Benchmarks of treatment progress are not beneficial in community interventions unless they are objective and verifiable. The stabilization of sleeping patterns can be objectively determined in a number of ways. First, people in recovery should keep a record of their sleep. Every morning, they can simply answer yes or no to the questions, "Last night did you fall asleep before 11:00 P.M.?" "Did you stay asleep all night?" and "This morning did you wake up before 7:00 A.M.?" More detailed questions can also be answered in a record of sleep regarding the perceived quality of their sleep, how well rested they felt in the morning, and whether they had trouble staying asleep after falling asleep. Surprise home visits in the middle of the night to users' homes can be very indicative about their sleeping habits. However, these are quite disruptive and can do more harm than good for people who are generally trying to sleep through the night without waking up. To individuals in recovery, it is important to frequently communicate just how important it is that they stabilize their sleeping patterns by going to sleep and waking up at a certain time. Sleep monitoring technology is available, and some of it is relatively inexpensive (i.e., *SleepTime* monitoring). However, monitoring generally measures patterns of disrupted sleep, which may be indicative of drug use, as opposed to measuring stable sleep patterns.

Verifying stable eating patterns can also be accomplished through self-reports. People recovering from meth addiction can help to demonstrate that treatment is working by reporting on a daily basis whether they ate breakfast, lunch, and dinner. In addition, people in recovery can be asked to provide food receipts and menu plans. Surprise inspections of kitchens can also tell quite a bit about a recovering meth addict's eating patterns.

Another critical measure of treatment progress is verified: distancing from key individuals. As long as individuals in recovery continue to associate with other meth users, it is difficult to imagine that they are going to be ready to stop using and that their treatment is working. Therefore, a benchmark of individuals' progress in treatment is staying away from those groups and individuals who are most likely to create relapse situations.

Verifying that individuals in recovery are staying away from key people who pose serious risks to their recovery is more difficult to establish. One way to start is to have people in treatment create a list of persons they know that they need to stay away from if they hope to stop using. This list can be reviewed with a trusted therapist or treatment confederate who would then help them develop plans of what to do if they happen to run into or speak to any of the people on the list. They can also role-play how they would respond to different situations when they might encounter people from their meth-using days. There is value to having them practice what they will say and do if they are accidentally exposed to or invited back into the meth-using culture. People in support roles can also make surprise home visits, which can be telling regarding the people with whom those in recovery choose to associate.

Verified stable daily living patterns, especially while individuals in recovery are living in their home communities, go a long way in establishing that treatment is in fact working. Stable daily living patterns, such as going to work and taking care of basic responsibilities and obligations, show that treatment has worked not just to get off of meth but also to begin making key lifestyle changes. These changes can be objectively verified because they usually involve other people and include things like work attendance, paying bills, and keeping appointments.

Finally, treatment progress can be measured not just by attendance at therapy sessions but also by whether individuals are actively taking advantage of their treatment experiences. This means that in addition to attending treatment sessions, people in recovery are also beginning to apply what they are learning in their treatment. Important as the participation of people in recovery in the treatment sessions might be, what is even more important is what happens between sessions. For this reason, quality outpatient treatment for meth addiction must always include homework assignments to be done between sessions. Community and family members can help to improve addicts' treatment experiences by asking the treatment providers about homework, to find out not just what the assignments are but also what are the intended effects of the assignments.

Outpatient treatment, even if it is intensive is still at most only nine to sixteen hours a week. This means that at the most, only 7 percent of an addict's time each week is spent in treatment. The rest of their time is spent living their life in their home community. While it may seem that the obvious solution to this would be to increase the amount of time they spend in treatment, doing so defeats the primary purpose of treatment. The primary purpose is to help individuals be able to live sober lifestyles in their home communities, and not be sober only during treatment sessions. Therefore, the better option is to help individuals begin practicing the sober living skills they learn in treatment. In addition, often some of the most important treatment exercises have to be done while individuals are at home in naturalistic settings for them to be able to work. Without the successful completion of many of these exercises, individuals in treatment for meth addiction may not receive all of the key treatment exercises needed for them to be able to fully recover from their addiction.

USE MONITORING

Abstinence monitoring is perhaps the most important of the measures of treatment progress since, regardless of how users in recovery may be doing at all of the other behavioral benchmarks, if they continue to use the drug, treatment is obviously not working. Monitoring substance use by individuals in treatment also helps assure that they are not just trading dependency on one addictive substance for another. Periods of verified abstinence can also be and are often used as mile markers for sobriety. The longer the individuals addicted to meth are able to abstain from using all addictive substances; the more likely they are to continue in sober lifestyles.

There are many ways to objectively monitor drug use. They all have one thing in common: they involve collecting some type of biological marker to determine whether or not there has been recent or past use of addictive substances. These markers can be trace indicators which provide evidence that there are drugs in the person's system, currently, or there have been some time in the recent or distant past. They can also be measurable physical signs of recent use, including coordination tests, sleep disruption, pupil dilation, and ocular motor tests. These measures of the physical signs of use are often used to determine that trace indicator tests have to be administered to clarify if in fact the physical signs can be attributed to drugs of abuse. Trace indicator tests include tests that establish that drugs of abuse are currently in a person's bloodstream and are likely to be producing signs of intoxication. These tests include blood tests and breath tests.

Urine tests are interesting in that while a positive test may mean that there has been recent use, they do not necessarily mean that individuals are still under the influence. This is because the substances that are showing up on the test are the drugs themselves or their metabolites that have already been removed from the bloodstream and are being released through the urine. However, a positive urine test does not necessarily indicate that individuals are *not* under the influence either. It is entirely possible that they had been using a drug for a period of time that is coming out in their urine and they continued using the drug and have it in their bloodstream as well and are currently under the influence. In comparison, saliva tests are somewhere in between blood and urine tests since the only way for drugs to get into saliva fluids is from the blood. However, just because drugs are found in the saliva does not necessarily mean that they are no longer in the bloodstream, since there is no process of metabolization, as there is before drug reach urine.

Methamphetamine is a psychostimulant drug that, generally speaking, leaves no trace indicators in blood or urine 72 hours after use. This presents some difficulties in use monitoring since tests that are too infrequent will miss use only because the drugs are out of the system before the test is administered. This means that quality urine testing for meth addiction must be administered at least twice a week and should be random and include weekends and holidays. One problem with random urine tests, however, is that the random schedule sometimes creates the very kind of relapse thinking that the person in treatment should be trying to change. A random schedule encourages at least the impression that if someone was tested on a particular day, it is unlikely that he or she will be tested any time too soon after that. Therefore, people who are being treated for addiction to meth and are on a random schedule for their urine tests, almost invariably, will experience an element of relapse thinking when they come in for a random urine test. Urine tests also can be fooled, and it is not uncommon for people addicted to meth who are being given random urine tests to explore how to dilute their urine, use someone else's urine in the collection process, or use other strategies designed to fool the tests. This is especially true if individuals continue to use and perceive that they have a lot to lose if they get caught.

For these reasons, quality use monitoring programs for meth addiction employ same-gender observed collections of urine that occur on a random basis on average twice a week. These quality programs also use some form of 24/7 monitoring to complement the urine tests. A distant past 24/7 monitoring test, such as a hair follicle test, provides information about drug use for the period of time the lock of hair tested was growing from the person's body. Administering a hair test once a month provides a verification of the urine tests done during the month. It also helps individuals in recovery not to have to struggle in anyway with thoughts that they can use without getting caught right after having done a test because of the perceived likelihood of their not being tested again in the near future.

Sweat patch tests monitor the presence of drugs released through the sweat glands during the period of time people wear patches and allow for 24/7 monitoring. This assumes that people wearing patches do not tamper with them.

One very interesting aspect about the sweat patch is that it is the only test that follows individuals around 24 hours a day and 7 days a week. That is to say, if individuals are adequately wearing sweat patches, then wherever they go they have a reminder that they are being monitored. For some people in recovery, this proves to be a very helpful tool.

Since use monitoring is at the heart any attempt to provide the structure needed for treatment to be successful, it is critically important to set up a use monitoring program that is reliable and valid. It is wrong to have people in treatment who use and then do not get detected because of a poor testing protocol. It is equally bad to have individuals who have not used be wrongly suspected of having used because of poor use monitoring programs.

Selling individuals on use monitoring is difficult to do, especially if their involvement in the testing is purely voluntary. If individuals are mandated by courts to do the use monitoring, then the question of whether or not they participate is much easier to answer. With people who are voluntarily receiving treatment, it is still important to secure their 100 percent compliance with use monitoring, since it is required for accountability. Whether individuals are seeking treatment voluntarily or are mandated to be involved in treatment, it is nonetheless important to discuss use monitoring as a necessary part of their treatment and as something with which they must comply. Taking a very nonjudgmental stance is important, so that they understand they are not being accused of lying or that they cannot be trusted. Those receiving the testing should be told that the entire purpose of the testing is so that they can be trusted because it would not be fair to them to put them in a situation of having to report when they used (if they did). This is because all that would do would be to create a setting in which they are motivated to destroy fragile feelings of trust in their loved ones. To some extent, being untruthful about drug use while individuals are in treatment can be normalized. This is because it is quite obvious that for most people, they have a lot to lose if their use is discovered. Abstinence monitoring, then, is nothing more than attempting to make it so that trust does not have to be hindered. The truth can always be found in the results of the very thorough and valid drug tests.

DAILY PLANNING

Another important part of structure is that people in recovery should be accountable for their time. Individuals who are in outpatient treatment may only feel the influence of their treatment during the actual treatment sessions. They may also be somewhat protective of their time and activities when they are not in session. However, unstructured time can be very dangerous since for many people boredom is a huge trigger for meth use. In addition, people in recovery have often led such disorganized and chaotic lives that they have likely developed very poor planning skills. For these reasons, daily planning is an important part of the structure needed for people to be successful in their attempt to recover from meth addiction. Daily planning also encourages them to have successful recovery thinking, such as taking recovery only one day at a time. Incorporated into their daily planning should be schedules for stable sleeping and eating, as has been described previously. Given the neurotoxic effects of meth on their brains that effect short-term memory and concentration abilities, daily planning also serves to remind meth users in recovery of important appointments and activities they need to be sure to attend.

RETENTION PLANNING

Finally, structure and accountability are important for a community-based treatment approach to be successful. They are important because it is necessary to help motivate meth users to stay in treatment even during a time when they may feel that they no longer need it. This is because treatment is likely to become most necessary and most helpful during times when they feel that they need it the least, perhaps because they are confident that they have their addiction beat. They may also believe that their addiction is something that they can truly put behind them. This is often only reinforced by friends, family members, and other supporters who themselves were so distressed by the addiction that they are ready to have it past them as well. However, this tendency is one of the noted critical bad judgments in the early stages of recovery. Structure and accountability become important parts of keeping people in early recovery in treatment before disaster strikes. Their own over-confidence, fueled by the false hopes of others who are seeking relief from the addiction almost as much as the addicted person, can give the impression that treatment is no longer needed. This is an error of judgment that can eventually lead to dropping out of treatment and to be at high risk of relapse.

By far the most powerful way to retain individuals in treatment is through a therapeutic approach called CM. CM is really nothing more than simply rewarding people for staying in treatment (see chapter 3). This works, in part, because it is clearly enjoyable for individuals in treatment to have some positive acknowledgement of their treatment efforts. What makes CM especially beneficial in the treatment of meth addiction is that it helps reinforce positive strides early in treatment, when many recovering meth addicts need it the most. Withdrawal from meth can create painful dysphoric mood states that can so easily be relieved with meth use that those in early stages of recovery have a high risk of relapse. In other words, in the early stages of recovery meth appears to those in recovery as a quick, easy, and effective treatment for feeling bad. Anything positive that has the potential of generating good and pleasurable feelings can be important during this stage of recovery. If what is positive is tied to the beginning stages of recovery, then the new association between the two can create a good positive momentum for individuals to continue in the recovery process.

The best reinforcers to use as incentives to stay in treatment are those things users identify as being enjoyable and important. An assessment of these things is necessary during the beginning of treatment, and it may involve talking to other people familiar with users' likes, especially since at that point users may not be able to identify with much not involving drug use which they truly enjoy doing. Therapists should develop schedules of reinforcing activities early in treatment and share these with clients at the very beginning of their treatment experience to keep them continually focused on the positive aspects of staying in treatment.

As has been mentioned, structure is what makes treatment possible. Treatment itself is really nothing more than some planned strategies that involve as many people from the recovering meth user's sober community as possible, all working together with a shared purpose and in a coordinated fashion. Treatment goals, while simple, represent the necessary changes that need to be made so that individuals in recovery stand the best chance of not returning to their meth-using lifestyle. The next chapter will discuss how community treatment teams help people recovering from meth addiction relearn how to experience pleasure and change some of their automatic beliefs and expectations about meth. The chapter also covers how to help them become meaningfully integrated into a sober social support group that will welcome them.

CHAPTER 6

Treatment

Returning now to the metaphor of sharpening an axe, one would remember that the sharpening stone in the case of meth addiction is treatment and the pressure to keep the axe pressed against the stone is the structure and accountability needed to make treatment possible. Structure, supervision, and use monitoring are all key ingredients for effective treatment but do not in themselves constitute treatment, any more than the pressure of holding the axe to the stone is in itself what will sharpen the axe. The spinning stone is what does the sharpening, and treatment comprises those methods of involvement in people's lives to help them make the key changes needed so that they are less likely to pursue their meth-using lifestyles. It was discussed in chapter 5 that treatment is most effective if it is community based. This is so that the burden of treatment is not borne by one individual or one agency and so that the influence of a sober community can offset the influence of the meth-using community. What exactly is meant by "treatment" is the topic of this chapter.

It has been mentioned that there are a number of changes needed in the lives of people addicted to meth, which, if not made, will almost certainly result in their continuing to use the drug and live in the drug-using lifestyles. These changes include distancing themselves from other people who use meth, establishing stable eating and sleeping patterns, learning to derive real pleasure from sober activities, changing automatic thoughts and expectations about meth, and building a number of meaningful relationships with other people who live sober lifestyles. Treatment is what is needed in users' lives to help these changes to come about. These changes can be divided into the familiar domains of biological, psychological, and social functioning.

Although they can be sorted in this fashion, it is important to remember that they are in fact interrelated and subsequently these changes occur as part of a holistic effort to adopt new sober lifestyles. It will become quite clear that treatment interventions and exercises, when creatively designed and implemented, can impact more than one area of change. Subsequently, efforts to effect change in one of the three domains can often be targeted to help with changes that are needed to be made in the other domains as well. Consider the following example:

> The drug court treatment team working with Esperanza was concerned that she may not be able to fulfill the requirement of the drug court that she eat three healthy meals a day mainly because they did not think she had learned the skills to purchase the food, plan the meals, and prepare the food. Furthermore, Esperanza's addiction to meth had led her to be neglectful toward her two small children ages one and three years. As a result, her children had been removed from her care and her involvement in the family drug court was part of her dependency and neglect treatment plan. The final goal of the family drug court treatment team was Esperanza's reunification with her two children, but they knew that food preparation and dietary management were not only important parts of her meth treatment but also important so that she could provide adequate care for her family.
>
> The treatment team decided that Esperanza needed help, and they made arrangements for two community volunteers, Carma and Dorothy, to take Esperanza to the grocery store so they could shop together for food. They showed Esperanza how to buy food for specific meals and how to shop for food that was on sale. They also purchased all of the food needed to prepare a chicken casserole and then went with Esperanza back to her apartment and made the casserole together. The whole time they were laughing and enjoying each other's company.
>
> When the meal was ready, they sat down and ate it together. The leftovers were stored in the freezer for a future meal, and Esperanza finished the evening understanding better how she can purchase and prepare food for herself and for her children. More important, she developed a close friendship with Carma and Dorothy, who started coming to her drug court hearings to show their support. Esperanza's treatment provider knew about the experience Esperanza had with the two volunteers and had her talk about how she felt meeting two new friends and how much she enjoyed being with them to prepare and then eat the meal. Esperanza shared with several people that the meal she had with her two "new grandma's" was the best time she remembers having for quite a while.

In this example, the intervention designed primarily to help a person in recovery stabilize her diet by teaching her some of the skills necessary for her to be able to eat three meals a day also helped accomplish other things. The treatment exercise helped Esperanza learn to associate feeling pleasure with something naturally pleasurable—enjoying a meal and the company of two new friends. Most important, the exercise served to help Esperanza to develop new friendships and support from the sober community, something that was critically important for her to be able to make the changes in her life she was trying to make. She needed to make these changes, so that she could get her children back and raise them in a safe and healthy environment.

BIOLOGICAL CHANGES

For individuals in recovery to be able to regain their maximum psychological functioning needed to live a sober lifestyle, they need to start eating and sleeping regularly. Helping individuals addicted to meth to begin doing this is quite difficult and challenging, especially in outpatient settings where there is little direct control over diets and sleep compared to inpatient settings.

The first step is to establish accountability and tracking mechanisms. It is impossible to know just how much change needs to be made and just how unstable these lifestyle patterns are without first having some kind of measurement of them. The accountability to keep track of these patterns will have the effect of changing them. When behaviors are tracked and measured, people become more aware of the targeted actions and they naturally start to change them because measurement of behavior is the first step toward change. Furthermore, it would be difficult to know if people are improving without establishing some kind of a baseline of the behaviors they are trying to change.

People recovering from meth addiction, especially during early stages of recovery, need to record every day what they had for breakfast, lunch, and dinner; what time they went to sleep at night; and what time they woke up in the morning. This can be accomplished by having them begin keeping a daily behavior-tracking log. While small notebooks will suffice, daily or weekly planners are better since they can be used so that they begin structuring their time as well. The use of daily planners will be discussed later in this chapter.

Once eating and sleeping patterns have been established using a tracking system, it becomes necessary to begin helping people to stabilize these foundational biological patterns, which became significantly disrupted with the abuse of meth. Helping them to stabilize their eating patterns is usually easier than helping them to stabilize their sleeping patterns. However, some people who are addicted to meth never learned the basic skills of making economic purchases of food, storing it, and then planning for its appropriate use to establish basic, stable, and healthy diets. In these cases, volunteers or others may be needed to help individuals learn the skills they will need to be able to begin eating better.

Food preparation and eating meals are very social activities that can be used as part of efforts to help users in recovery integrate with a sober community as well. A helpful strategy is to have them prepare and submit menu plans such as the weekly diet plan. For many individuals this will be difficult to do in the early stages of recovery, so assistance and participation from other sober community members will be important to have. Supervising individuals, such as drug court judges, probation officers, or human services case workers can also ask them to submit food receipts showing their attempt to purchase food and stabilize their diets. Every opportunity to consult with dieticians or nutritionists should be taken, especially because so many of the health problems while individuals are using meth and while they are in the early stages of recovery are due to poor dietary habits.

Stabilizing their sleep patterns is quite challenging since prolonged meth abuse has been linked to a number of sleep disorders. For meth users, patterns of sleeping become erratic and unscheduled when using because the drug decreases the need for sleep. The thirst for excitement while intoxicated leads people under the influence of meth to seek out stimulating activities, in lieu of resting. If they do sleep while under the influence of meth, it often is non-sustained and non-restorative because the sleep tends to be short and frequently interrupted. Sleep that occurs following periods of binge use, which is often described as "crashing," is deep and lasting but still non-restorative because it is mainly a sign of exhaustion and forced recuperation. As a result, when people addicted to meth stop using and then try to establish normal sleep patterns, it is often a very difficult thing to do. It is difficult because they are neither physically nor psychologically accustomed to falling asleep at certain times in the evening. The opposite tends to be true because when they were using meth, nighttime was a cue for heightened activity and energy. Instead of feeling tired and sleepy at nighttime when sober people are going to bed, people recovering from meth addiction often feel awake, alert, and experience insomnia.

In addition, because the only prolonged sleep often obtained while actively using meth was that which occurred during extended periods of "crashing," users in recovery are not accustomed to waking up at a certain time after they have fallen asleep. Proper sleep "hygiene" is one of the first steps toward establishing sober lifestyles. A sleep "hygiene worksheet" can be very helpful. The purpose of a worksheet (log) is to first help identify the common sleep problems people in recovery typically experience. Then, once these problems have been adequately identified, people in recovery can then start tracking their sleep patterns for at least seven days using the sleep log. In the log a record can be generated of all the relevant factors, describing sleep experiences and tracking those things that are most likely to be having a negative impact on sleep. Therapists and people in recovery can then discuss strategies for learning to fall asleep and for developing the ability to stay asleep. Finally, people in recovery who have sleep problems can use their worksheets to develop a personal plan for improved sleep hygiene. In the plan they can describe their exact sleep problems, explore the reasons they are not sleeping well, and plan how they will use the strategies to improve their sleep experiences.

DAILY PLANNING

Time management is another necessary part of treatment for people in recovery for meth addiction. Time is an interesting concept relevant to meth addiction because for people who become involved in heavy meth use, time begins to become a blur of chaotic experiences. The simplest measure of the passage of time is day turning to night and then to day again. If individuals are abusing meth, nights and days start to meld together since there are few or only erratic interruptions of conscious experience through sleep. Subsequently, people addicted to meth often report losing total track of time in terms of days spent high and using, numbers of days spent crashing, and experiences that occur at night or those that occurred for them during the day. For this reason, an important part of treatment for people addicted to meth is the structuring of their time.

Structured time starts with tracking days by the simple act of sleeping at night and then waking up to a new day. Then as people begin to stabilize and to sleep normally, they can and should plan specific times they will go to sleep at night and specific times they will wake up in the morning. Planning is also important for establishing bedtime and morning rituals, which become important parts of stabilizing sleeping patterns. Individuals can also plan when and what they will eat on a daily basis to assure that they are eating three healthy meals a day and are meeting the necessary dietary requirements of their recovery-based treatment plan.

After people in recovery have adequately planned for their sleep and for their meals, other aspects of their time can and should be structured. These include things like planning to be able to show up for work on time, planning for travel, and showing up on time for important appointments, such as meetings with a probation officer or a drug court judge. People in recovery need to plan everyday how they will interact meaningfully with some people from their sober network of friends, family, and other supportive individuals. They should also plan for at least one sober activity everyday that brings them feelings of pleasure simply by doing that activity. The activities do not have to be overly extravagant. In fact, they are more effective when they are simple and require very little preparation or planning. Obviously, these sober activities will be most rewarding and therapeutic when they are engaged in with supportive friends from the sober community. Those in recovery can indicate which activities interest them the most, and those activities can be the ones they are encouraged to engage in first. Examples of sober activities might include the following:

- Attend a church meeting
- Attend an AA or NA meeting
- Attend any kind of sobriety-oriented support group meeting
- Clean something
- Collect anything interesting to you
- Do an act of service for your neighbor
- Do something fun outside
- Do yard work
- Get active in a public cause
- Fix something for another person
- Get around to doing anything you have always intended to do
- Go for a drive
- Go for a walk
- Go to a movie
- Go for a workout
- Go window-shopping
- Learn a skill
- Make a favorite food
- Play with your children

Unstructured or unfilled time is a dangerous thing for people in recovery. For many people addicted to meth, boredom is a relapse cue because they used meth as a way of creating excitement in their lives. Meth is a stimulant drug, and it is very effective at making even the most boring and mundane situations seem exciting. Therefore, for an outpatient treatment experience to be successful, they must be accountable to someone who has sanctioning power over them regarding the structuring of their time and the ways they are spending their time.

Perhaps the most important activity to be monitored through adequate planning is staying away from other people who continue to use meth. People in recovery should be accountable to report a list of 10 people whom they must stay away from if they hope to discontinue their use of meth. They should have a ready plan for anyone working with them to review regarding how they intend to stay away from these people.

A difficult issue with daily planners and behavior tracking logs is to know for certain if individuals in recovery are doing the tracking on a daily basis or if they are simply entering information at the last minute to please whomever it is they are reporting to. A way of making certain that the planners are being used on a daily basis is to have individuals call a number everyday and listen to a message that they are expected to record in their daily planners. The message could be changed everyday so that they would have to record every new message. This represents a measure of whether they are at least opening their planners and writing in them everyday. Hopefully, as they do this they will record their eating and sleeping patterns as well.

An added benefit of having them call everyday to listen to a recorded message is that the messages can also be used as indicators of when they need to submit to randomly scheduled drug tests. They could be told beforehand which particular message they are to listen for, and when they hear that message, they would know if they need to provide a urine, saliva, blood, sweat, or hair sample that day. Traditionally these recorded "indicator" messages have tended to be assigned colors. However, using assigned sobriety oriented statements instead of colors has the added benefit of engaging them in an exercise of considering sober thinking patterns on a daily basis. Having them record these messages in their planners not only helps assure that they are calling in every day but also helps them to consider a different message everyday. Table 6.1 shows some examples of sober statements that could be used.

In an ideal daily planner, individuals should write their names on the front of their planners as well as the week to which the planner applies. The first page of the planner is where they should record their sobriety statement, or true expectation, as well as the number they are to call every morning to see if they need to provide a test for that day. They should also write down on the first page of their planners the address of the drug-testing agency so they know where to go to do the test.

The planner should contain a list of people they should not be around because of the risk they pose to sobriety. The list should be developed by them and those working with them. Discontinuing contact with people who continue to use meth is a critical part of successful outpatient treatment. They are expected to write specifically what they will do to avoid any of the people

Table 6.1
Daily Sober Statements for Call-In Program

	Day of the week	Sober statement	Statement assigned to client indicating the need to drug-test that day
First week	Monday	Remember, your sobriety matters, *you* matter.	
	Tuesday	Living sober may be tough at times but it is worth it.	✓
	Wednesday	Life without meth and other drugs gives me freedom.	
	Thursday	I don't have to do this alone. There are others who care.	
	Friday	Life is better without meth.	
	Saturday	Living sober may be tough at times but it is worth it.	✓
	Sunday	I don't want to trade what I have gained for anything.	
Second week	Monday	Living sober may be tough at times but it is worth it.	✓
	Tuesday	Just for today I am going to stay sober.	
	Wednesday	Living sober may be tough at times but it is worth it.	✓
	Thursday	Sobriety has helped me see my worth as a person.	
	Friday	I feel better now than I ever have.	
	Saturday	I am realizing how good it is to not be using meth.	
	Sunday	Living sober may be tough at times but it is worth it.	✓

	Day of the week	Sober statement	Statement assigned to client indicating the need to drug-test that day
Third week	Monday	Nothing is more important than my sobriety.	
	Tuesday	I have found true joy.	
	Wednesday	Living sober may be tough at times but it is worth it.	✓
	Thursday	If I trust and believe, I can achieve.	
	Friday	Meth is not who I am.	
	Saturday	Stay humble and realistic, especially about sobriety.	
	Sunday	I know I can do it if I allow others to work in me.	
Fourth week	Monday	Living sober may be tough at times but it is worth it.	✓
	Tuesday	Step by step and day by day, I can stay sober.	
	Wednesday	My true friends are those who support my sobriety.	
	Thursday	I can decide each moment of everyday to stay sober.	
	Friday	Living sober may be tough at times but it is worth it.	✓
	Saturday	Everyday gets better when I am sober.	
	Sunday	Remember, you are worth it.	

from their list if they should happen to run into any of those people or if they should happen to call.

On a daily basis, people in recovery should keep track in the planner of all relevant information regarding their sober activities, their eating and sleeping habits, the sober statements they call in and listen to, and how they feel about themselves and their sobriety. The planner should contain a daily log for all of this information. They are expected to enter this information daily.

In addition, they should be expected to plan out every hour of their day from the time they wake up until the time they go to sleep.

An interesting addition to a use-monitoring program, which uses twice-a-week random urine drug tests and monthly hair follicle drug tests, is the daily use of the sweat patch. The patch, when worn properly, detects drug use through chemical tests of the sweat left on the patch during the time that it was worn. Chemical analysis of the patches is quite expensive, but the patches are relatively cheap. To enhance their sense of accountability and ownership of their recovery process, patches can be given to individuals to have them put on themselves at the beginning of each day. At the end of the day, they can remove the patches, place them in a chain-of-custody envelope, and then sign an affirmation statement, which they put in the envelope with the patch. The affirmation statements can be nothing more than small pieces of paper on which they write a statement at the end of the day reaffirming their commitment to stay sober. At the end of each week, they can be held accountable to turn in seven of the patches and daily affirmation statements in their chain-of-custody envelopes. Those working with individuals in recovery who are wearing the patches can then decide which, if any, of the patches they would like to send to the lab to be tested.

Obviously, individuals can manipulate the patches by tampering with them or by not even wearing them because they are the ones responsible for putting them on and taking them off each day. That is actually not that big of a deal as long as, in addition to the patch, they are also doing twice a week random urine drug screens and monthly hair follicle tests. The patches are really for them, and they can be a tremendously helpful tool for them to stay sober, if they choose to use them. The patch is a daily reminder that stays with individuals throughout the day helping them to remember to live sober. The patch also adds an element of accountability that most individuals do not expect—being accountable to themselves. If they do decide to wear the patch and to not manipulate it even though they could, it is a step in the direction of personal commitment to stay sober and to work their recovery program.

PSYCHOLOGICAL CHANGES

There are a number of psychological factors that affect the continued use of meth by even the most motivated individuals. None is more powerful than the positive, although untruthful, expectations from the drug and the conditioned response people addicted to meth experience over time. Expectations are thoughts people have that effect behaviors almost immediately. Even if a certain behavior has not produced a positive or desirable outcome in the past, if it is expected that it will in the future, then the behavior will be performed. This helps shed light on the reason why people continue to engage in behaviors that are clearly harmful and that seem to have no real gain or benefit. The use of meth is a good example of this. With all of the negative and seemingly unwanted effects of meth use on appearance, health, and overall psychological well-being, it would seem that people who use meth would stop because it is hurting them.

There are a number of other unpleasant outcomes from meth use so that it would seem people who were using it would want to stop. These include things like family problems, legal entanglements, reoccurring incarceration, poverty, lack of stable housing, no job, and negative peer associations. With all of these negative effects, the rational approach would be that users would see they are related to their meth use and then stop using no matter how good it feels in the short run. The flaw in this reasoning is the assumption that active meth users attribute the negative things happening in their lives to their use of meth. The reason this is not a safe assumption is that there can be many other forces and events that can be blamed for the negative outcomes. Users only need to be creative in attributing these negative elements to things other than meth. For example, they may blame others, such as the courts, family members, friends, or the police for the negative things that are happening to them.

More specifically, rather than realizing that it is the meth that is causing so many problems with the law, users instead attribute their problems to law enforcement officers who are persecutory and unfair. Rather than attributing the removal of children from their parents due to meth use and how it negatively affects users' ability to care for their children, it is easier to instead blame child protection caseworkers or community members who reported on them. If users believe that their use of meth is not causing them problems and that instead it is what makes life exciting for them or at least makes life bearable, then they will continue to use. They will use in spite of whatever negative consequences they may experience. That is how powerful their expectations can be.

Negative expectations about sobriety or about users' ability to live without meth also affect attempts to stop using. People addicted to meth do not always see that it is the meth that is causing all of the negative problems in their lives. They do not expect that they would be able to stop using and stay sober. They may also expect that life would be too boring or intolerable without the meth. Consequently, people having these expectations continue to use meth. They will continue even knowing that bad things are going to happen to them from their meth use.

Expectations are powerful, and they are difficult to change because for most people they happen almost automatically. People have expectations that can cause certain behaviors to occur without critical thinking. This is because expectations are really nothing more than thought habits that we use to anticipate consequences of our behavior. We are always judging what we think the outcome our actions may be, and these are our expectations. If they are inaccurate, we do not seem to mind too much as long as they are right at least part of the time. This is really a matter of selective remembering. For example, people addicted to meth maintain false expectations about meth by simply paying attention to only those bits of information that support what they would like to believe about their drug use. That is, they believe it is not that big of a deal, everyone else they know is doing it, and they can stop whenever they want. They simply have not decided that they want to stop.

Meth users may also believe that that they are using it by choice because they are bored and it helps them to focus. They are unlikely to remember the times when they had been using meth for several days at a time and became paranoid and terrified and then began to hide from shadows and non-existent threats. For meth users, misattributed expectations can be convenient ways of thinking about such behavior as to make change seem unnecessary. This way of thinking tends to only be reinforced by meth use because the drug infuses users with a false sense of power, capability, and competency. They are even less likely to believe that there is anything wrong with what they are doing because their thinking is so distorted by meth and cannot believe that anything bad is going to happen to them.

While changing expectations about the drug and about sobriety is hard work, it is not impossible. Changing expectations correctly is an important part of treatment. In fact, part of the discomfort, because of which people addicted to meth may not want to stay in treatment, is created by the realization that their beliefs and expectations will have to be changed. This means that they have to acknowledge their weakness and inability to manage their addiction to meth. This important first step in treatment is not all that dissimilar to the first of the 12 steps of Alcoholics Anonymous and Narcotics Anonymous, which is, "We admitted we were powerless over our addition/over alcohol—that our lives had become unmanageable." For users in treatment, this is bound to involve some pain and discomfort as changes need to be made. This is not at all unlike what it might feel like to be the axe held against the sharpening stone, as the spinning stone knocks off the rust and the corroded metal to produce a sharpened edge.

The first step to changing expectations involves generating a more truthful and realistic perspective on the effect of meth on people's lives. As was mentioned, this may be uncomfortable for users. Skilled therapists or community treatment participants will have to help users ease into these realizations, as opposed to expecting that sudden and full confrontation will produce self-blame and desire change sufficient enough for the users to seriously seek sober lifestyles. The process of uncovering the lies people addicted to meth may tell themselves about the drug and what it has done to them should be progressive and should involve multiple strategies.

A helpful strategy is to simply have them start to represent some of their false beliefs about meth by creating collages using pictures, words, and drawings. The purpose is to have them express many of their false expectations in pictures and images first, before having them try to express themselves in words. It is also important that the false and true expectations that they come up with be their own and not something from other people. Irrational expectations are as personal as our gait. That is, our own individual way of being and our thoughts are much the same way. Collages are good places to start in helping people addicted to meth identify their false and true expectations because they are not cued in any sort of way. They have to be generated from the individuals themselves. Later, words and phrases can be used to help them describe some of their false beliefs about meth. However, if they start with a prepared list of false and true expectations, there is risk that they will simply choose from the list as opposed to coming up on their own with phrases describing how they really think.

Contrasting collages can be especially beneficial for comparison purposes. For example, individuals in recovery can start by making two collages, one that represents what they expected a meth high to be like right before they started using and then another collage that represents what their high would turn into after they had been using a while. Next, they can do two more collages, one regarding what they thought about meth when they first started doing it and then another representing what they found out meth was really like after they had used it for a while.

Once collages have been used to generate ideas regarding unrealistic and false expectations of meth, users in recovery can be helped to begin putting words to their thoughts. This may require that they are cued and then respond with their thoughts, beliefs, and expectations. For example, they can be asked to describe in writing the details of what it was like for them the first time they tried meth. Then, they can be asked to write the details of how they feel about meth now that they have become addicted. They might also be asked to describe in detail their worst experience using meth. Then they can be asked what they now plan to tell themselves about meth, the next time they think something like, "Just one more use isn't going to hurt."

The purpose of the collages and of the written paragraphs about expectations of meth is to help them ultimately generate their own list of false expectations they used to have about meth and the true expectations they now have about it. The false expectations can be considered lies people tell themselves about meth so they will keep using it. The true expectations can be considered the clarifying thoughts they can use to dispute any of the lies about meth they might find themselves thinking. Table 6.2 displays examples of some typical false and true expectations about meth use.

As was previously mentioned, it is critically important that the expectations be from the individuals in recovery and that they be true representations of their ways of thinking about meth. Skilled therapists can help them find the right expressions for their automatic thoughts, not by giving them examples but by getting them to talk openly about their using experiences. Therapists can then help them to remember the things they would think about their use, especially right before starting to use. Therapists must monitor the physical signs of cravings to help those who may have urges to use as a result of these exercises. Those physical signs are also good indicators that the thoughts they have identified are actual expectations they have had about using. Therefore, if individuals begin to show and/or express cravings as a result of the thoughts they are discussing, thoughts such as, "Man, when I am bored and I got money, I want to light it up," then those thoughts are likely to be expectations they have that lead to use.

The goal of CBT is to help people change the irrational thoughts they have about themselves, their environment, and their future that are creating concerning behaviors. A quick look at the false expectations people addicted to meth have about it helps shed light on just how powerful these thoughts can be. If they think and believe that they cannot have fun without meth, that meth will make all of their pain or problems go away, or that their meth use is not a problem, and so on, then it is likely they will continue using. Helping people addicted to meth change expectations such as these is an important part of the psychological treatment for meth addiction.

Once users' personal false expectations of meth have been successfully identified using some of the previously mentioned strategies, the next step is to help them to change them. The difficulty in doing this is that often these expectations do not exist as conscious verbal thoughts. People addicted to meth may not even realize they are having these thoughts. Instead, they tend to form very quick almost unperceivable automatic impressions and judgments that govern behavior without their realizing that they are thinking them.

Table 6.2
False and True Expectations of Meth

	False expectation	True expectation
1.	I get stuff done when I am high on meth.	I am unproductive when I am high on meth.
2.	Meth makes me look good.	I look like death when I am on meth.
3.	I can't live without meth.	I can live without meth.
4.	The only way I can have fun is by using drugs.	Real fun is better than drug fun.
5.	No one really cares about a meth addict.	People care about me.
6.	I use meth so I can get things that I like.	Meth will make me lose everything that is important to me.
7.	I use meth so I can keep people who are important to me.	I will lose everything and everyone that is important to me if I don't stop using meth.
8.	I like meth. Some people like to drink, well, I like to use meth.	It doesn't matter what other people like or don't like. I can't use meth.
9.	I am a meth addict, so this is what I do.	I am in recovery so this is how I stay sober.
10.	Meth is going to make all of the pain go away.	Meth only causes me more pain in my life.
11.	I can do meth only once and it is not that big of a deal.	Doing meth "only this one time" over and over got me to where I am now.
12.	Sure I use meth, but I am not as bad as other tweekers.	Who am I kidding, I was just as bad as other tweekers or on my way to becoming like that.
13.	I'll only do this for meth, just this once.	I haven't been able to do anything for meth, "just this once."
14.	My true friends understand that people use meth, so what?	My true friends understand what meth was doing to me and want to help me be sober.
15.	I can walk away from meth whenever I want to.	I am kidding myself if I think I can just walk away from meth whenever I want to.

Table 6.2 (continued)

	False expectation	True expectation
16.	Some people drink, I use meth, who cares?	Other people may be able to drink or use drugs. I can't.
17.	Nothing feels as good as a meth high.	Nothing feels as good as being sober.
18.	I have got to use something to deal with life. That's why I use meth.	I can deal with life sober and it sure feels good when I do.
19.	I can use meth now and take care of my responsibilities later.	Using meth makes it so I don't take care of my responsibilities.
20.	Meth doesn't hurt me.	If I continue to use meth, it will end up killing me.
21.	I am just one of those people, a meth addict.	I am a sober person.
22.	If I am going to use meth, I may as well do it good.	"Going out in a blaze of glory" means I die. What's so cool about that?
23.	I may use meth again, I may not.	It is always better not to start using meth again.
24.	I use meth because I choose to.	I used meth because I became addicted and could not stop.
25.	I can't trust anyone unless they use meth.	I can't trust anyone who uses meth.
26.	It's no big deal to just get high on meth this once with a few friends.	Stay away from people who use meth. Period.
27.	People in recovery are cowards who couldn't handle the "high life."	Recovery takes courage. Cowards fantasize they can control their meth use.
28.	Meth helps me talk to people.	I am crazy when I'm on meth. People don't like that.
29.	I can't handle meth cravings. They are too strong.	I have handled many things well in my life. I can handle meth cravings too.
30.	I guess I just wound up being a meth addict.	A tweeking meth addict who can't stop. That's not who I want to be.
31.	Sometimes I just use meth. I don't know why.	I can plan my life so that I don't use meth.

	False expectation	True expectation
32.	Sober people don't care about me.	There are many sober people who are pulling for me.
33.	I'll stop using meth and just smoke pot or drink.	I want to be sober from *everything*, not just meth.
34.	If I don't use meth, I won't keep people in my life.	The people I bring into my life when I use meth, I don't want anyway.
35.	Life without meth is boring.	Living sober is thrilling and it feels good.
36.	If I want to be close to some people, I have to use meth.	When I am using meth, I am not really all that close to anyone.
37.	The first time I used meth, it was the greatest feeling I have ever had.	It *never* feels like the first time. That "first high" is just a stupid fantasy.
38.	Nothing is better than sex on meth.	Sober sex is *always* better than meth sex. Here's why…
39.	Meth will make my problems go away.	Meth only makes my problems worse.
40.	I am good at getting high on meth.	There is nothing admirable or respectable about using meth.

Therefore, the step of accurately identifying the personal thought and impression habits of people addicted to meth is often difficult to do. It requires patience and persistence but is, nonetheless, necessary. Trying to help people change their impressions cannot be done until their personal automatic thoughts have been accurately identified.

Assuming that this has happened, they should have a list of at least 10 false expectations they have had about meth that have led them to use it in the past. They should also be able to identify whether these expectations are true or false. Therapists or community members should not do this for them. However, fellow addicts in treatment may be able to help them see the truth behind their lies. This is because their shared experiences will likely make it easy for those in recovery to trust each other and give accurate interpretations about their beliefs about meth.

It is important not to assume that all expectations regarding meth are necessarily false, although most are when considering lasting effects and negative consequences. But an expectation such as, "I can make money selling meth" may be true. Some individuals may have been able to make money selling meth, so it would be inaccurate and ineffective to produce change to try to convince users in recovery that this is a lie they tell themselves. Instead of using "I can't make money selling meth" as their true expectation, their true or sober expectation may have to be something like, "Yeah I could make some money selling meth, but I wouldn't hang on to it long and before I knew it, I'd be broke again."

People in recovery need to have true and sober expectations that they themselves have helped generate that speak the truth to them about what their meth use was really like. For every expectation that led to their using, they need a sober expectation that tells them the truth about what using meth does to them. The next step in their treatment is then to help them so that every time they have a using expectation, they automatically replace it with their sober or true expectation. It is important that this is rehearsed repeatedly so that it becomes as automatic for them to have the sober expectation as it is for them to have the meth-using expectations.

There are exercises that can be used to help make this happen. Some of these exercises will need to be done during therapy sessions with a skilled therapist, but other exercises should be practiced everyday in between sessions. These between-session exercises are perhaps the most important, since they are to be applied when they are living their day-to-day lives outside the protective environment of therapy sessions.

Other psychological changes to be accomplished as part of treatment have to do with conditioned responses associated with pleasure. In effect, for people addicted to meth, the drug hijacks their pleasure response. The addictive properties of the drug, its effect on pleasure, and the associations that are developed all result in users feeling good and not feeling bad because of using the drug. For meth users, it becomes all about the drug. Meth users tend to lose the ability to feel good about things that naturally feel good. They also lose the ability to relieve themselves from bad feelings. The drug does these things so powerfully that it becomes the primary tool for turning on good feelings and for turning off bad feelings.

An important part of treatment, then, is to help people addicted to meth to establish healthy associations between feelings of pleasure and naturally pleasurable experiences. It is also important that they break their learned association of using meth and feelings of pleasure. It is almost like playing a matching game in which they are learning new associations between pleasurable feelings and the kinds of experiences that naturally produce those feelings.

Treatment exercises to help meth-addicted people to learn these associations can be quite rewarding, and are most effective when they involve sober people from the community who are willing to participate. In essence, treatment teams working with users in recovery need to see how important it is to help them begin to experience pleasure because of things that are naturally pleasurable. The best way to do this is to reward their progress in treatment with opportunities (exercises) to engage in pleasurable activities with people from the sober community. These exercises are designed to have the effect of modeling for them how to experience pleasure from naturally pleasurable activities. Individuals can then be asked to report in treatment what they witnessed and how it felt for them. Not just therapists but all members of the community-based treatment team can take part in helping them to process the pleasure of doing these activities by simply making them aware of what individuals in recovery are doing and then asking them about it. They can also discuss with those in recovery how the pleasure of engaging in these activities compares with how they felt when they were using meth. They should be asked to be honest. There will be something about their meth use that they enjoyed. These aspects about their use should not be discounted, or they will be insufficiently considered and could cause relapses down the line. The goal is to help them begin to recognize the differences between natural pleasure and induced pleasure that comes from meth use. Even if they do still associate meth use with intense, immediate pleasure, users in recovery can be helped to learn that lasting pleasure from natural experiences can be more rewarding because there is no bad "aftertaste."

These "pleasure recalibration" exercises are limited only by the creativity of the community-based treatment team. While it is an excellent strategy to use these experiences to reinforce treatment progress, these experiences can and should also be ordered as part of the mandated treatment experience. This is because users in recovery are not always going to expect that the experiences will be pleasurable and that they should be made to engage in them nonetheless. An important part of their treatment is that they explore many different sober activities to experience pleasure.

> Veronica was very hesitant to go to a community dinner event that had been recommended by her treatment provider, but the treatment team decided it was important that she go. The drug court judge ordered her to attend, and then she reluctantly agreed to go. Veronica and two other women in the drug court were treated by the community to a day of pampering before the event. They went to a local salon, and the owner donated free manicures, pedicures, and hair styling in preparation for the event. Then, the three women were treated to new clothing outfits from a women's clothing retailer. They were accompanied throughout the day by several people who were hosting the event, and everyone became more and more excited about the dinner as the day wore on.

That evening Veronica and the two other drug court participants enjoyed a fine dining experience and were approached and warmly greeted by many members of the community. They were surprised by special recognition prizes that were given to them by the organizers of the dinner. Veronica and the other women had been asked to come to the front of the room, where they were given their prizes and were acknowledged as being "special community change agents." The next week in drug court Veronica tearfully expressed to the treatment team that she had "the time of her life" and that she felt she had made some new friends and acquaintances as a result of the dinner whom she hopes to stay close to for some time to come.

Sober community volunteers become an important part of these experiences and can also help identify sober activities in which those in recovery can be involved since it is best to have them be simply invited to go along with sober volunteers to do pleasurable activities the volunteers enjoy doing anyway.

Community safety should be the highest priority when involving local community organizations and volunteers in the treatment experiences. It is also important that the people selected to participate in the activities with those in recovery be carefully screened to maximize the possibility of a positive experience for everyone involved. They must also be trained so they understand not just how they can participate but also why their participation is so critical. With a sense of purpose, community volunteers are much more likely to participate in a way that is congruent with the community-based treatment plan. With pleasure recalibration exercises, community volunteers act much more as treatment confederates or partners than as simple support volunteers. For this reason, it is important that they understand the theory of community-based treatment so that they can understand how to participate in the treatment exercises in ways that help bring about the targeted outcomes.

Communities can be of significant help in supporting people in recovery by providing sober activities and opportunities for recalibration. Some examples of pleasure recalibration activities or exercises that were designed to help meth users become integrated with a sober community are mentioned below:

- A select group of meth users in recovery were given the opportunity to go on a "ballooning journey" with a local ballooning club that offered to take them free of charge. The community participants were a sober ballooning crew who served nonalcoholic beverages in lieu of wine as part of their voyage.
- Two users in recovery were invited to help a local car club obtain and begin restoring a classic car. The level of trust shown to them by the

car club turns out to be as significant as the work they did. Community participants were members of the local auto restoration club, which was informed about the program, what was being attempted, and what special precautions they should take to prevent any kind of avoidable mishaps.

- People in recovery had a meal at a local restaurant. The community participant was a restaurant that donated the meal and community volunteers, who gladly went with the individuals in recovery to help "model" for them how to enjoy a fine meal. No alcohol was served during the meal, and the users in recovery were asked to write about the different foods they had eaten and to turn in their log to the drug court judge.
- A local cycling club offered to take two users in recovery on a leisurely 10-mile bike ride. The community participant was a local cycling club. The club provided the bikes and all the gear for them to be well outfitted for the ride. Then they offered to help them line out their own bike and gear if they decide that riding is something that they would like to keep doing.

SOCIAL CHANGES

Helping meth users in treatment make key changes in regard to who they associate with is perhaps the most difficult therapeutic task to accomplish. It is difficult because their choice of who to have around them is not just theirs to make. Quite often, even when people in recovery are actively trying to make changes in the composition of their social group, there may be people from the using community who make this difficult for them. This could be for a variety of reasons. One reason is that people in recovery often pose a threat to those who are continuing to use. This is because those who are still using are paranoid and suspicious due to the effects of the drug. In addition, they are concerned that those friends who have stopped using and are trying to change will turn them in to the authorities. For this reason, it is often difficult for people who are still actively using to leave people who are trying to stop alone. Sometimes even with the best intentions to distance themselves from other people who are actively using meth, people in treatment for meth addiction cannot always control whether or not they are still influenced by the powerful social dynamics of the using community. It is for these reasons that a community-based treatment model targets these social changes as a direct goal of the treatment team. It is still the people in treatment who are burdened with coming up with who it is that they need to stay away from, but people from the sober community can offer help in the way of support. They can also provide suggestions of things they can do or say to people who are still using when they happen to run into them or when they call.

The pleasure recalibration exercises already discussed can go a long way in helping get users in recovery more actively involved in a sober community, especially when there is an active attempt on the part of the treatment team to include sober volunteers in those activities. The accountability of having to report to a judge, other governing forces, or individuals who they need to avoid and what they will do if they happen to run into any of these people also helps make the social changes needed. In addition, there may be treatment exercises they need to complete to plan what they will do and what they will say to try to distance themselves from people still actively involved in the meth-using community and to integrate meaningfully with the sober community. Most of these treatment exercises should involve the rehearsal of what they plan to say and what they plan to do if/when they interact with people from the using community.

Individuals may need to practice writing out planned responses before they practice actually saying the words they would use to turn away an ex-friend, spouse, romantic partner, associate, or whoever has continued to use meth and/or hang out with other people who continue to use it. In some cases, they may need to send out an announcement or a note informing most people who know them that they are in recovery and that they do not intend to be around substances of abuse anymore, nor around people who use them. For example,

> "Hey, how's it going? Look, I've been meaning to tell you. I have just got to stay away from you because_____."
>
> "This might sound mean, but I've been thinking about what really matters to me and I've decided to stop using meth. That also means I've got to change who I hang out with. Please help me by_____."
>
> "Meth plus me equals disaster. I want to change. You can help me. Please don't try to see me or contact me. I am sorry, but if you do I will _____."

Those individuals in treatment for addiction to meth need to plan how they are going to stay away from other people who continue to use the drug. They should also plan to stay away from people who abuse any kind of drug or alcohol. In addition, they should also plan how it is that they will become involved with people who do not abuse drugs or alcohol. Rather than waiting for them to figure this out, there may have to be some attempts made by the treatment team and the sober community to facilitate this happening since they often have no idea how to go about doing it. In many cases the sober community has to be brought to them as opposed to it being the other way around. This may be the most challenging component of community-based treatment, but it is also one sure to bring the greatest success to those who would stop using meth and stay away from it entirely, if they had a sober community that would welcome them.

CHAPTER 7

Getting Started

For families and communities invested in helping people addicted to methamphetamine stop using the drug and begin living sober lifestyles, the obvious place to start may seem to be getting individuals identified and then engaged in treatment. However, it makes no sense to dive right in without a clear plan of how to use the principles presented thus far so that treatment can be maximally beneficial. Like most things in life, good treatment begins with good preparation. Because of the level of involvement of so many different components of the community, preparation is much more than simply identifying a plan for treatment. The programs, systems, and processes needed to effectively do community-based treatment must be in place long before clients are engaged in the therapeutic process.

For communities, action planning and practical steps to address meth use begin at the grassroots level of defining the problem as it exists and then moving forward with a targeted response. In its basest form, addressing the problem of meth addiction begins by simply stating that communities can be basically divided into two groups: those who have used meth and those who have not. Of course, the approaches with each group will differ. For those who have used meth and have since stopped, primary prevention is about helping them to never go back to using. Secondary prevention is done with those who have never tried meth but who are considered to be at high risk to start. Those populations at highest risk to start using include disenchanted adults from lower socioeconomic backgrounds who tend to abuse alcohol and marijuana already; children, especially adolescent children, with parents who are active users of meth; and adults with general coping-skill deficits who have turned to substance abuse as a way of dealing with their problems. Secondary prevention involves helping the general population, which is made up of those who may or may not be identified as at risk of trying meth, to avoid using in the first place.

Important as prevention is, however, these interventions are often inadequate in helping those who are already addicted to meth. Unless a community program began before meth use has grown into anything significant, prevention does little to help people who are actively using the drug. Users will require the help of the community to facilitate effective treatment that works. The general community action steps to help people who are actively using meth include (1) identification, (2) involvement, (3) engagement, and then (4) treatment.

IDENTIFICATION

For communities struggling with meth addiction, it may seem that identifying those who are hooked on the drug is an easy thing to do. That may be true of the "low hanging fruit" addicts who are easy to recognize because of their involvement in community systems. However, those people represent only a select few of the population who are part of the meth addiction problem. Finding and identifying others may require more work, and it may not be something that is quickly or easily accomplished. The key agencies involved in the identification process include law enforcement (both investigative and drug task force work), health-care providers, county or local departments of human services (more specifically child protection services, adult protection and welfare fraud), and other concerned members of the community.

People in need of help are also sometimes self-identified, such as when individuals tell a physician, teacher, employer, friend, or mental health counselor that they are addicted to meth and that they need help trying to stop. More commonly, they are identified by a spouse or other concerned family member who sees the problems that meth addiction has caused in a loved one's life and then decides to tell someone. Reports of problematic use are just one step, however, as it becomes necessary to verify and to investigate the exact nature of the problem before identifying the person as needing treatment. It is always possible that the report provided is an exaggeration of what may actually be the case.

INVOLVEMENT

Once enough evidence suggests that a person is using meth, then it may be sufficient to conclude that something needs to be done. This is because current use of any amount can be concerning since (1) it is likely that the use that is identified is only a small portion of what the person is actually doing and (2) even initial use of the drug can very quickly turn into strong addiction. Helping meth users at that point to become involved in a community-based intervention really means catching them so that the structure and discipline of the treatment system can be put into affect. In criminal situations, law enforcement officers build cases that demonstrate evidence of use, manufacturing, and/or distribution of the drug. Prosecutors then establish convincing reasons for conviction on which judicial officers then eventually make a ruling. However, not all criminal cases that involve meth are directly related to drug manufacturing, use, or distribution. Many times meth use is determined to be a significant mitigating factor in cases in which the primary crimes committed were things like check fraud, identity theft, burglary, shoplifting, and/or domestic violence.

> Terri was a 32-year-old woman who was considered to be a well-known meth user in her community mainly because of the people she had been associating with since her arrival in the community 5 years earlier. The man with whom she was residing had been arrested several times for domestic violence related to incidents that involved his previous girlfriend. While it could never be established, law enforcement officers had always been suspicious that this man used meth and that his use of it played a part in these cases. Terri herself had charges of petty theft from the jurisdiction in which she lived before moving to the community. Terri's case acquired a new dimension when she was implicated in a felony theft offense. Terri worked as a home health nurse, and she was accused of having stolen over $5,000 worth of cash and valuables from people she helped take care of, most of whom were elderly and vulnerable adults. Prosecutors in her case argued that she was addicted to meth and that she stole to support this habit. Terri's attorney did not deny that she had used meth but argued instead that only because of her use of meth was she around the people who had taken advantage of her situation. Other users actually had been stealing items from the people with whom she was working.

In such cases, prosecutors and defense attorneys must figure out how to bring the evidence suggesting meth use into central consideration so that rulings can also address the meth use as a significant goal of the sentencing arrangement.

There is a little more flexibility for involvement in cases of child neglect or maltreatment. When it can be established that a parent uses meth, this is usually enough evidence for child protection case workers to open a dependency and neglect case involving the family. However, at some point suspicion of use has to be replaced with clear and convincing evidence of the parent's level of use and how their use has negatively impacted their ability to adequately parent their child or children. In many cases, it is simply presumed that if a parent uses meth, then they are maltreating their child or children even if there is no evidence. It can be assumed that even if no maltreatment has occurred, the risk that it may happen is simply too high. The risk can be about the behavior of other meth-using adults that invariably become a part of the child's life since the parent has to get their meth from someplace and from someone. The risk can also be about what the parent may or may not do while under the influence. It is always preferable that there be a direct and irrefutable tie established between the parent's drug use and their parenting behaviors. With this tie firmly established, it is much easier for treatment systems to begin working with these parents since the issue of why they need to be involved in treatment is indisputable. Meth-using parents can also be helped to see that the key for them to be with their children is to become and stay sober, since it was the drugs that affected their parenting, and not because they themselves are incapable of loving their children and of being good parents.

ENGAGEMENT

Engaging people in treatment raises the very interesting question of whether people addicted to meth have to choose to be in treatment or if they can be forced by others to do so. The assumption is that for treatment to be effective, it has to be something people choose for themselves. In the case of court-ordered treatment, however, this is not true since the structure, accountability, and supervision provided by a coerced treatment experience provides essential elements for it to be effective. In cases involving family members or others who are not involved with judicial systems but were forced into treatment by concerned others who are close to them, things are often not quite so simple. This is mainly because there really is no easy system of structure or accountability already set up in these relationships. Instead, this has to be created by those working with the people addicted to meth. For family members and others who are trying to create the needed structure, a big challenge can be developing the sanctions and rewards necessary to motivate addicts to engage in treatment.

Sanctions are tricky with people who are not involved with the legal system primarily because there are no ultimate sanctions available that involve containment and the loss of freedom like incarceration. There are times when users in early stages of recovery need the containment and separation that incarceration affords. The most powerful sanctions that can be used by family members and loved ones working with people addicted to meth actually come from good planning. That is because the most effective sanctions are those that involve the removal of planned rewards.

> Laura's family knew how to keep her motivated to stay involved in a community treatment program for meth addiction, and struggled to do so. Laura had expressed what seemed to be sincere desires to engage in the program, to distance herself from other people who used meth, and to stop using meth herself when she first started the program. However, in spite of what her family members, therapists, and others were saying to her, she began missing treatment sessions, skipping assignments, and expressing to everyone that she was convinced that she did not need to continue with treatment. She stated she got everything out of it that she needed to stay sober.
>
> Her family had made it a habit of surprising her with some kind of a meaningful family activity to celebrate each week she completed in the program. These activities included things like a dinner at a restaurant with sober friends from Laura's childhood whom she had not seen for years, going to the movies together as a family (something she had enjoyed doing before she started using meth), and family members spending one-on-one time with her talking about what it meant to them that she had stopped using.
>
> Laura had known for some time that her family planned to help her to get her driver's license back once she completed one month of treatment. Laura was told that she needed to keep attending every session of treatment and doing the assignments so that she could get her license back. She was also told that if she would stay engaged in therapy for another week by attending all sessions, doing all assignments, and not using, they would also take her to go look at used cars, and she was planning on buying a car with their help.

Perhaps the greatest struggle for families and communities helping people addicted to meth who are not court-ordered into treatment is the realization that they may ultimately lose their personal relationships with the meth addict. When these personal relationships involve loved ones, the struggle becomes more difficult. Forcing a meth addict into treatment can result in their fleeing or breaking off all contacts with family members and the sober community. The question becomes, is it worth it for loved ones to try to force people into treatment if doing so means that they will flee their loved ones and cut off all contact with them? This is something only the family members can decide for themselves. However, in making this decision, the family may want to consider what they have to lose by forcing the person into treatment, causing him or her to reject or cut off all contact with them. It may be that family members do not have much to lose, because they did not have much contact with them anyway. If they did have some contact, that could be lost if the meth user who is being forced into treatment decides to flee the relationship, as opposed to engaging in treatment. The loved ones have to realize that even if they had not confronted their loved ones and tried to force them into treatment, the loved one may have fled the relationships anyway. Family members should also consider what might happen if they do nothing versus what would happen if they confronted their loved one who chose to flee the relationships. At least trying something is often easier for families of meth addicts as opposed to not doing anything and watching the person's life just wither away.

TREATMENT

Once people using meth have been identified, caught, and then are motivated to not only go to treatment but also to do the assignments associated with their therapy, they can start receiving the treatment they need to stop using. This treatment will involve helping them to make new sober associations and feel welcome in the sober community, change their expectations about meth, and begin feeling good about things that are naturally pleasurable.

COMMUNITY ASSESSMENTS

Communities beginning to put together plans to address meth can use this simple framework to assess how well they are doing at addressing the different aspects of meth use. A representative team of professionals and others from the community, if they are convinced that meth addiction is a problem in their community, can be brought together to review progress and what needs to improve. With each of the stages of identifying, involving, engaging, and treating people, representatives from the community can assess how well their community has been doing and then identify areas they think they might improve.

STEPS TO DEVELOP COMMUNITY-BASED TREATMENT

The steps to develop a community-based treatment model are outlined in the following paragraphs:

Step 1: Identify and recruit key players. Individuals and agencies needed to develop a community-based treatment approach include treatment providers (both private for profit and public nonprofit); supervising individuals and agencies (i.e., child protection case workers, judges, probation officers, employers, etc.); collaborative support services (legal consultants, employment specialists, physicians, leaders from the faith community, people from mutual support groups, and housing specialists); family members; employers and/or potential employers.

Step 2: Check egos and political agendas at the door. Members of a community-based treatment team will need to be able to work collaboratively with one another. To do this, it will be important that the goals of the team are never hampered by alternative agendas of the team members.

Step 3: Establish healthy and effective group norms. Treatment team members need to buy into shared approaches for handling the tasks of the team. This includes staying focused on the outcome; manifesting investment in group purpose through between-meeting work, and planned discussion items; avoiding "subgrouping"; and showing mutual respect and need regardless of stature in the community.

Step 4: Develop communication pathways. Group e-mails, conference calls, and in-person meetings can all be effective ways of communicating regarding treatment team issues. It is important that time and resources be invested into making face-to-face meetings enjoyable but, more than anything, productive.

Step 5: Pool resources. Resource gathering is likely to be a big challenge for teams. It is important not to depend on "soft money," money that comes primarily through grants. The old adage of "use it up, wear it out, make it do, or do without" is quite applicable as the team will need to get used to doing the best they can with what they have, as opposed to waiting until the ideal is available. Perhaps the best resource is that of good "money-getting" people; those people who are good at writing grants and at securing funding to assure the sustainability of a program. It is important for the team to remember that their most important resource, even more important than money, is the time invested by team members. Therefore, the time of team members must be respected and never wasted.

Step 6: Identify strengths and limitations. It will be impossible for the treatment team to "save" every addict every time or solve every community problem. The community-based treatment program cannot be all things to all people, but it can be a dedicated group with a clear vision of purpose, direction, and course of action. It can also be the synthesis of all members working together as the whole is always greater than the sum of the parts.

Step 7: Develop plan for program participant identification and enrollment. The entry point for potential program participants must be defined, and a plan put into place for screening. Specifically, it is important that exclusionary and inclusionary criteria be established to determine who gets admitted to the program and who does not. Determination must also be made regarding who it is that will be doing the screening and whether or not they have the necessary training and background to do them. They must also be well trained in all of the specifics of the program.

Step 8: Develop a plan for regular reporting of treatment progress to supervising individuals. Objective behavioral benchmarks as well as general treatment progress indicators should be used, and there needs to be standardized reporting procedures in place to avoid the appearance of favoritism. In addition, participants need a system in place to report on accountability factors.

Step 9: Identify reporting/appearance frequency and process. Contact maintained by the person in treatment with the governing individual or agency that has sanctioning and reward-giving abilities is the key to the structure and accountability that will help make treatment successful. This contact can be lessened as participants progress through the program, although caution should be exercised not to withdraw these contacts too quickly. If individuals are doing exceptionally well and the contacts are helping to provide the structure and the accountability, then it may be better to have contacts continue for a while longer. The strategy should be to increase frequency of visits as needed without making them punishing but be conservative and only use them as required by circumstances.

Step 10: Identify the strength and the structure of the supervision. What is it that participants have to lose for failing to make progress in the program? What do they have to gain? These incentives can be used to move forward, but they can also be used to place structure on their experience. Participants should take part in the contingency development, but the treatment team should be the one to decide when and how both sanctions and rewards are administered, so that the prescribed effect is all part of the treatment plan. Plans must be put in place to administer both sanctions and rewards as quickly as possible following targeted behaviors so that the greatest effect will be achieved.

Step 11: Collaborative assessments. Plans must be developed for intake information sharing to assure quick yet comprehensive assessments.

Step 12: Regular monitoring of stability and ongoing case management. Case management is the work needed to aid program participants in taking care of their basic needs. Without this help, there is always the potential that participants will become distracted from the therapy because they do not have the ability to take care of themselves or their dependents. There is no harm in always checking first things first, nor is there harm in being redundant. Harm will happen in a community-based treatment approach if is there are no or too few community support workers who are willing to "roll up their sleeves" and help with the sometimes dirty work of case management.

Step 13: Regular "huddle" meetings. Regular meetings of the treatment team are necessary so that skilled treatment providers can describe to the teams their strategies and approaches for each particular stage of the participants' recovery. There must be open discussion and review of treatment plans as well as a chance for all community participants to express their views on areas still in need of treatment. Sometimes the participants themselves can and should be invited to these meetings.

Step 14: Plan for ongoing program assessment and improvement. Data collection regarding the effectiveness of the program is important not only to track the progress of program participants but also to hold the program itself accountable to an expected outcome. Many lessons can be learned from a virus. One is that a virus is not ignorant of its environment. It cannot help but be aware of challenges from the environment, because its principle form of survival is adaptation. Likewise, community-based treatment programs should embrace outcome data, because it can inform treatment teams about what is working and what is not working. The accountability measures for program participants can act as the needed outcome data to indicate if the program is working and which aspects of it are still in need of improvement.

A case example of an effective team that implemented some of the previous components is the following:

> The criminal drug court in a small rural county had been in existence for about eight years and had survived perhaps its greatest challenge, four years ago, changing the judge who heard the drug court docket. Now, the treatment team felt things were running smoothly, and of those who started the program, there seemed to be a decent percentage that also completed it. However, the team was anxious to improve the program and had decided to introduce more stringent measures of progress in the program as opposed to just the results of occasional random drug tests. After initiating a stricter procedure for monitoring sleeping and eating patterns, the team began to notice that they could predict which clients were going to start missing treatment sessions and then eventually start testing positive for drug use based on the stability of eating and sleeping patterns. They then began conducting mandatory weekly sleep hygiene and nutritional planning workshops for all participants. Sleep patterns began to stabilize, and clients, in general, began eating more regularly, and even eating more nutritious meals. Ongoing assessment of treatment progress showed that fewer clients were missing sessions and fewer were producing positive drug tests.

WHERE TO START FOR FAMILIES

Family-based interventions with no legal or outside involvement have the advantage of allowing the family and the person seeking help to have total control over their the treatment plan. The disadvantage of family-based treatment models with no outside community involvement is that sanctioning and structuring becomes more difficult to do and will almost inescapably become intertwined with the relationship dynamics of other family members. That is because, in the family, there really cannot be one truly objective governing body. In these cases, decisions typically made by a drug court judge or a probation officer need to be made by more than just one family member. In fact, the healthier the family members who can participate on the treatment team, and the more truly concerned and completely sober they are, the better. In these cases, decisions are made by the whole team, and not just by one person. If one family member or loved one decides to take on the task for him/her, they are likely to become completely overwhelmed with the responsibility and their relationship with the addicted individual will not escape some kind of effect, usually a negative one.

Family members working together to intervene in the meth use of a loved one should broaden their pool of invested participants to include sober and healthy close friends and other community members. The message to be sent by family members is the same, namely, that there is a sober community that exists and that it is interested in the user's sobriety and well-being. Clear expectations of change and involvement in therapy must be communicated to the meth-addicted family member headed toward recovery and there must be clear and strong boundaries supporting those expectations from everyone participating on the treatment team. All other aspects of community-based treatment for meth addiction can be the same. The only difference between volunteer family members in treatment and volunteer drug court participants in treatment is that if drug court participants get off track, then they have the judge to ultimately answer to and they will inevitably be doing some jail time. If volunteer family members get off track with their treatment, then they face whatever sanctions the treatment team can formulate to help them to stay for the entire duration of their outpatient program. If users start with inpatient treatment, then the family members need to make sure that a solid plan for outpatient community-based treatment, including a treatment team and a competent treatment provider. This provider must be willing to participate collaboratively as part of the treatment team.

Families need to be healthy and to have intact and well-functioning healthy boundaries. The treatment provider can help the family assess these characteristics of their treatment team and, if needed, can do family therapy so that interfamilial conflict, splitting, and playing favorites do not interfere significantly with the work of the team. Regular involvement in Alcoholic Anonymous (12-step mutual support groups for families of alcoholics and addicts) and working through the steps are very wise initiatives and should be considered by any family deciding to attempt a family/community-based treatment response.

CONCLUSION

One thing seems to be certain about methamphetamine and about what it takes to help people who become addicted. That is the social and community aspects of addiction to meth and to treatment introduce a whole new way of approaching an individual behavioral disorder, such as substance dependence. This new approach challenges traditional treatment models by design. It is community inclusive and has the primary purpose of treating addiction by helping meth users become meaningfully integrated into a sober and supportive community. The effect of this approach is not limited to whatever benefit it might have for people addicted to meth, because true community-based treatment also requires that participating communities address and then resolve many of the biases that exist about people who use drugs and those who are in recovery. Communities need to hold those addicted to meth accountable and involved with the sober community. These can be two critical components of successful treatment. The very act of initiating these efforts in sober communities will help people have more personal perspectives on what meth addiction means and what is needed for those addicted to be successful in recovery. Compassion, concerns, expectations of accountability, structure, and support can serve to heal fragmented relationships between people addicted to meth who are trying to recover and the sober communities they once may have shunned and who once may have shunned them.

The broad awareness about a drug like meth and common familiarity with once heavy users who are trying to turn their lives around can impact communities by "de-monsterfying" people with meth addiction problems. At the same time, users can help to educate community members about the drug and about what needs to be done to help prevent future use by others within the community. This "double effect" of community-based interventions that help with treatment and prevention maximizes the impact of a very concentrated effort to not only help with current addiction problems but also prepare the community to avoid future problems.

Changes in people who were once addicted to meth but are living sober and have meaningfully integrated with a sober group of caring people can be paralleled with changes in the community itself. A recent media campaign out of Multnomah County, Oregon attempted to educate the general public about meth and its effects on users by showing pictures of people who became addicted to meth before their addiction worsened and then after they had been using heavily, usually only for a short period of time. The differences in appearance are striking and the comparative pictures are often used as part of prevention efforts to show just how devastating meth use can be (see http://www.drugfree.org/Portal/DrugIssue/MethResources/faces/index.html).

Unfortunately, this slide show also communicates that addiction to meth is a dead-end street and that people who have started using are not going to stop until they are either completely incapacitated or dead. Those who have been using meth are portrayed as having been irreparably damaged with little hope of complete recovery. While there are many cases of people who do stop using meth and who become healthy and productive members of their communities, the Faces of Meth slide show does not seem to convey this hope.

Faces and Voices of Recovery, on the other hand, is a national nonprofit campaign that attempts to advocate for people in recovery (among many other ambitious purposes) by reaching out to communities about the possibilities of recovery from addiction to alcohol and other drugs, including methamphetamine. Their message is one of hope as they attempt to show the personal faces and stories of so many people who have been successful at discontinuing patterns of addiction and who are living sober and productive lives. Community-based interventions, when successfully employed, can help add to this effort as more people become sober from meth use and as more community members become aware of their changes, offering support along their path of successful sobriety.

Perhaps it would make sense to aid Faces and Voices of Recovery in their attempt to counter many of the negative biases that result from campaigns such as Faces of Meth by showing the "Faces of Communities in Recovery." While the "before" shots (such as those shown in the Faces of Meth campaign) would be of what people and their communities look like when they are in the throws of meth addiction, the "after" shots could be of people who were once addicted to meth living sober and meaningful lives and deeply involved with a sober community that they care about and that cares about them.

Appendix

Examples of Studies of Evidence-Based Treatments for Stimulants, Cocaine, or Methamphetamine Use

Contingency management		
Design	**Results**	**Source**
Methadone maintenance patients showing evidence of cocaine use were exposed to two one-week reinforcement conditions. Patients could earn $50 vouchers for meeting urine sample requirements twice a week on Wednesdays and Fridays and on Mondays, $100 if their samples were clean.	Participants were more likely to meet the requirements (abstinence) on Wednesdays and Fridays, and following the weekend on Mondays. However, the results found that the shaping reinforcement condition did not increase rates of abstinence on the final abstinence test.	Correia, C.J., Sigmon, S. C., Silverman, K., Bigelow, G., and Stitzer, M.L. 2005. A comparison of voucher-delivery schedules for the initiation of cocaine abstinence. *Experimental and Clinical Psychopharmacology* 13 (3): 253–58.
A study of 100 cocaine-dependent outpatients assigned to either community reinforcement or community reinforcement plus vouchers.	Combining county reinforcement with vouchers had therapeutic value on substance abuse during treatment and at posttreatment follow-up, but the effects for cocaine	Higgins, S.T., Sigmon, S.C., Wong, C.J., Heil, S.H., Badger, G.J., Donham, R., Dantona, R.L., and Anthony, S. 2003. Community reinforcement therapy for cocaine-dependent

Contingency management		
Design	**Results**	**Source**
	use were limited to the treatment period.	outpatients. *Archives of General Psychiatry* 60 (10): 1043–52.
Treatment staff, patients, and administrators were interviewed to determine if CM had any positive effect on treatment, staff morale, patient motivation, and other important factors.	A variety of sources were used such as letters from patients, records, videotaped interviews, and interviews with staff, patients, and administrators found that the use of CM increased patient motivation for treatment and recovery, facilitated treatment progress and goal attainment, improved attitude and morale of staff, and developed a sense of affirmation among all involved. The authors acknowledge the limitations of their approach and observations.	Kellogg, S.H., Burns, M., Coleman, P., Stitzer, M., Wale, J.B., and Kreek, M.J. 2005. Something of value: The introduction of contingency management interventions into the New York City Health and Hospital Addiction Treatment Service. *Journal of Substance Abuse Treatment* 28 (1): 57–65.
A study of 159 cocaine-abusing adults who had been randomly assigned to a CM treatment, classified on the basis of whether they had participated in three or more family-related activities during a 12-week treatment period.	Results indicate that participants who were involved in family activities remained in treatment longer, were abstinent for more weeks, and reported lower family conflict compared to participants who did not engage in family activities. The data suggest that participants who participate with their families during CM treatment have better	Lewis, M.W., and Petry, N.M. 2005. Contingency management treatments that reinforce completion of goal-related activities: Participation in family activities and its association with outcomes. *Drug and Alcohol Dependence* 79 (2): 267–71.

Contingency management		
Design	**Results**	**Source**
	outcomes and lowered family conflict.	
This study evaluated the effectiveness of low-cost prize reinforcement CM for reducing cocaine use. 120 cocaine-using patients in a community-based treatment program were randomly assigned to one of three 12-week treatments—standard treatment, the same treatment with incentives up to $80 or $240.	The study found that patients in the $240 incentive group obtained more abstinence than those with no incentives. Those who entered treatment with clean samples continued their abstinence regardless of which group they were assigned. The authors propose that CM may be suitable in community-based settings and benefits may vary by magnitude of initial cocaine use at entry into treatment.	Petry, N.M., Tedford, J., Austin, M., Nich, C., Carroll, K.M., and Rounsaville, B.J. 2004. Prize reinforcement contingency management for treating cocaine users: How low can we go, and with whom? *Addiction* 99 (3): 349–60.
Study of 142 cocaine- or heroin-dependent outpatients randomly assigned to standard treatment, standard treatment with vouchers, or standard treatment with prizes for 12 weeks.	Findings indicate that CM outpatients stayed in treatment longer and achieved greater lengths of abstinence than did standard treatment patients. Abstinence did not differ at 6- and 9-month follow-up periods. The best predictor of abstinence was the longest period of treatment. The prize and voucher approaches were virtually equal in long durations of abstinence.	Petry, N.M., Alessi, A., Shelia, M., Marx, J., Austin, M., and Tardiff, M. 2005. Vouchers versus prizes: Contingency management treatment of substance abusers in community settings. *Journal of Consulting and Clinical Psychology* 73 (6): 1005–14.
Low-cost CM was evaluated in its efficacy in reducing cocaine use and attendance in group	The CM group submitted more clean samples and attended more treatment sessions than the standard	Petry, N.M., Martin, B., and Simcic, F. 2005. Prize reinforcement contingency management

Contingency management		
Design	**Results**	**Source**
therapy. Patients were randomly assigned to 12 weeks of standard therapy or standard therapy plus CM. Patients assigned to the second group became eligible to win prizes ranging from $1 to $100 for clean urine screens.	treatment group. The best predictor of abstinence at follow-up was the duration of abstinence during treatment.	for cocaine dependence: Integration with group therapy in a methadone clinic. *Journal of Consulting and Clinical Psychology* 72 (2): 354–59.
This study evaluated the effectiveness of CM in eight community-based treatment settings. The study randomly assigned 415 cocaine or meth users to standard treatment (usual) or standard treatment plus abstinence-based incentives for a 12-week period.	Participants in the CM group remained in treatment longer, attended more counseling sessions, had more stimulant-free samples, was more likely to achieve 4-, 8-, and 12-week abstinence benchmarks than the control group. But, both groups submitted a low number of positive samples. The authors conclude that CM improved retention and abstinence results.	Petry, N.M., Peirce, J. M., Stitzer, M.L., Blaine, J., Roll, J.M., Cohen, A., Obert, J., et al. 2005. Effect of prize-based incentives on outcomes in stimulant abusers in outpatient psychosocial treatment programs: A national drug abuse treatment clinical trails network study. *Archives of General Psychiatry* 62 (10): 1148–56.
Study randomly compared treatment as usual with treatment as usual and CM for a 12-week period. Participants submitted urine samples over the course of the study.	Participants who received CM and treatment as usual submitted more substance-free urine samples than those who only received treatment as usual. CM patients on average maintained their abstinence for almost five weeks compared to almost three weeks for the treatment-as-usual group.	Roll, J., et al. 2006a. Incentive-based therapy improves outlook for methamphetamine abusers. November 6. www.nida.nih.gov/ newsroom/06/NR11-6 .html.

Contingency management		
Design	**Results**	**Source**
Seventeen methadone-maintained cigarette smokers received four weeks of CM as a stop-smoking intervention.	Results indicated that CM patients significantly reduced breath CO levels from baseline to completion of treatment and that 23.4% of patients maintained one week or more of continued smoking abstinence. Results indicated a link between smoking abstinence and reduced cocaine use, although not reduced opiate use, which raised questions about possible shared biological and psychological mechanisms for tobacco and cocaine use.	Shoptaw, S., Jarvik, M.E., Ling, W., and Rawson, R.A. 1996. Contingency management for tobacco smoking in methadone-maintained opiate addicts. *Addictive Behavior* 21 (3): 409–12.
This study of a small sample of clients studied whether abstinence supported by periodic reinforcement might carry over to non-reinforcement periods and enhance rates of cocaine abstinence among methadone maintenance participants.	Clients receiving incentives achieved significantly more cocaine abstinence on incentive days compared to non-incentive days.	Sigmon, S.C., Correia, C.J., and Stitzer, M.L. 2004. Cocaine abstinence during methadone maintenance: Effects of repeated brief exposure to voucher-based reinforcement. *Experimental and Clinical Psychopharmacology* 12 (4): 269–75.
Patients in a methadone maintenance treatment program were allowed to draw from a fishbowl if they provided cocaine-free drug screens or if they had attended group sessions.	The CM subjects provided twice as many negative drug screens as the control group over a 12-week span. They had a group attendance rate of 70% compared to the control group's 30%.	Petry, N.M., Martin, B., and Finocche, C. 2001. Contingency management in group treatment: A demonstration project in an HIV drop-in center.

Contingency management		
Design	**Results**	**Source**
	Low-cost prize-based systems are effective in getting patients to attend treatment and pass drug screens.	*Journal of Substance Abuse Treatment* 21:89–96.
This study tested what happens when escalating value of vouchers (CM) was eliminated after three months of treatment, where patients received escalating rewards for compliance. Patients were randomly assigned to experimental and control groups.	After eliminating the escalating CM, the CM group demonstrated a decline in clean cocaine or opioid drug screens. The authors conclude that there is a need for more intensive psychosocial interventions during CM treatment.	Kosten, T., Poling, J., and Oliveto, A. 2003. Effects of reducing contingency management values on heroin and cocaine use for buprenorphine and desipramine-treated patients. *Addiction* 98 (5): 665–71.
This study tested whether CM via vouchers made a difference in participation, and abstinence among cocaine-dependent clients.	Study found that 75% of cocaine-dependent clients who received CM which included vouchers for drug-free samples and counseling completed their 24-week trail compared to only 40% of those receiving counseling only. CM clients also had longer periods of abstinence than non-CM clients.	Higgins, S.T., Burdney, A.J., Bickel, W.K., Foerg, F. E., Donham, R., and Badger, G.J. 1994. Incentives improve outcome in outpatient behavioral treatment of cocaine dependence. *Archives of General Psychiatry* 51:568–76.

Contingency management and cognitive-behavioral therapy		
Design	**Results**	**Source**
A study of 193 cocaine-using methadone maintenance outpatients randomly assigned to 12 weeks of group therapy (CBT or control group) and voucher availability (CM contingent on cocaine-negative urine or noncontingent).	During treatment preliminary CM effects were dampened by cognitive-behavioral treatment. However, following treatment there were additive benefits of cognitive-behavioral and CM.	Epstein, D.H., Hawkins, W.E., Covi, L., Umbricht, A., and Preston, K.L. 2003. Cognitive-behavioral therapy plus contingency management for cocaine use: Findings during treatment and across 12 month follow-up. *Psychology of Addictive Behaviors* 17 (1): 73–82.
This study directly compares the efficacy of CM with cognitive-behavioral and combined therapies among stimulant abusers; 171 stimulant-dependent participants were randomly assigned to three groups for a 16-week treatment period. CM participants received vouchers for stimulant-free urine samples.	CM produced better treatment retention and lower rates of stimulant use during the study period. At follow-up, stimulant use did not differ among the three groups at follow-up. CM displayed the strongest effects during treatment, but cognitive-behavioral demonstrated greater effects over the long term. The study found no evidence of an additive effect when CM was combined with cognitive-behavioral treatment. The authors report that CM has a more robust treatment effect for reducing stimulant use during treatment and is superior to CBT. CBT also reduces stimulant use and has comparable results at follow-up.	Rawson, R.A., McCann, M.J., Flammino, F., Shoptaw, S., Miotto, K., Reiber, C., and Ling, W. 2006. A comparison of contingency management and cognitive-behavioral approaches for stimulant-dependent individuals. *Addiction* 101 (2): 267–74.

Contingency management and cognitive-behavioral therapy		
Design	**Results**	**Source**
A study of 120 patients with cocaine dependence who were receiving methadone maintenance treatment randomly assigned to one of four conditions: CM, CBT, combined CM and CBT (CBT + CM), or treatment as usual (i.e., methadone maintenance treatment program only [MMTP only]) ($n = 30$ per cell). The active study period was 16 weeks, requiring 3 clinic visits per week. Participants were evaluated during treatment and at 17, 26, and 52 weeks after admission.	Urinalysis results during the 16-week treatment period show that participants assigned to the two groups featuring CM had significantly superior in-treatment urinalysis results, whereas urinalysis results from participants in the CBT group were not significantly different from those of the MMTP-only group. At week 17, self-reported days of cocaine use were significantly reduced from baseline levels for all three treatment groups, but not for the MMTP-only group. At the 26-week and 52-week follow-up points, CBT participants showed substantial improvement, resulting in equivalent performance with the CM groups as indicated by both urinalysis and self-reported cocaine use data. Study findings provide solid evidence of efficacy for CM and CBT. Although the effect of CM is significantly greater during treatment, CBT appears to produce comparable long-term outcomes. There was no evidence of an additive effect for the two treatments in the CM + CBT group.	Rawson, R.A., Huber, A., McCann, M., Shoptaw, S., Farabee, D., Reiber, C., and Ling, W. 2002. A comparison of contingency management and cognitive-behavioral approaches during methadone maintenance treatment for cocaine dependence. *Archives of General Psychiatry* 59:817–24.

Contingency management and cognitive-behavioral therapy		
Design	**Results**	**Source**
This is a study of combining CM with a cocaine-specific relapse prevention approach (cognitive-behavioral) for 61 cocaine-using patients in a methadone maintenance program. Participants were randomly assigned to one of four treatment approaches for eight weeks plus an eight-week follow-up period.	CM was significantly related to reduced cocaine use and the counseling module to six-month retention rates. Both CM and the counseling module were related to positive outcomes for participants.	Rowan-Szal, G.A., Bartholomew, N.G., Chatham, L.R., and Simpson, D.D. 2005. A combined behavioral intervention for cocaine-using methadone clients. *Journal of Psychoactive Drugs* 37 (1): 75–84.
A randomized study of gay or bisexual men who were involved in meth use and high-risk behaviors. It compared four treatment approaches, including cognitive-behavioral, CM, a combination of the two, and a culturally tailored CBT.	The results indicate statistically significant differences among the four approaches. CM and cognitive-behavioral with CM showing the best results. Significant reductions in meth use and high-risk sexual behaviors were obtained.	Shoptaw, S., Reback, C. J., Peck, J.A., Yang, X., Rotheram-Fuller, E., Larkins, S., Veniegas, R. C., Freese, T.E., and Hucks-Ortiz, C. 2005. Behavioral treatment approaches for methamphetamine dependence and HIV-related sexual risk behaviors among urban gay and bisexual men. *Drug and Alcohol Dependence* 78 (2): 125–34.

Matrix model		
Design	**Results**	**Source**
A multisite outpatient study that compared treatment as usual with the Matrix model, which is a manualized 16-week treatment method.	The study found that in most sites, those patients assigned to the Matrix model participated in more clinical sessions, stayed in treatment longer, provided more clean-urine samples, and maintained longer periods of abstinence than the treatment-as-usual groups. The study lends support to the efficacy of the Matrix treatment model over the usual treatment.	Rawson, R.A., Marinelli-Casey, P.J., Anglin, M. D., Dickow, A., Frazier, Y., Gallagher, C., Galloway, G.P., et al. 2004. A multi-site comparison of psychosocial approaches for the treatment of methamphetamine dependence. *Addiction* 99:708–17.

Medications		
Design	**Results**	**Source**
This study compared the efficacy of the compound bupropion hydrochloride and CM for reducing cocaine use in 106 opiate-dependent cocaine-abusing (methadone-maintained) individuals. Participants were randomly assigned to four treatment groups of CM and placebo, CM and bupropion, voucher control and placebo, or voucher control and bupropion.	The groups did not differ in baseline or retention rates. Opiate use decreased significantly with all groups attaining about the same levels of opiate use at the end. For the CM and bupropion group, cocaine-positive samples declined significantly and remained low for many of the weeks. The findings indicate that combining CM with bupropion has more improved outcomes than bupropion alone.	Poling, J., Oliveto, A., Petry, N.M., Sofuoglu, M., Gonsai, K., Gonzales, G., Martell, B., et al. 2005. Six-month trial of bupropion with contingency management for cocaine dependence in a methadone-maintained population. *Archives of General Psychiatry* 63:219–28.

Prevention		
Design	**Results**	**Source**
Self-report study examined the long-term effectiveness of universal preventive interventions on meth use by adolescents during their late high school years. Participants in two comparison groups were sixth- and seventh-grade rural school students who were tracked to see if prevention efforts were effective through the Iowa Strengthening Families Program and the program with additional life skills training. Self-reports of lifetime and past-year meth use were collected over a 4½- to 6½-year span for the groups.	The two groups both had significantly lower reported use rates than the control groups. The program and life skills training both had significant effects on lifetime and past-year use. The results suggest that universal interventions have the potential to reduce methamphetamine use among adolescents.	Spoth, R.L., Clair, S., Shin, C., and Redmond, C. 2006. Long-term effects of universal preventive interventions on methamphetamine use among adolescents. *Archives of Pediatrics and Adolescent Medicine* 160:876–82.

Community reinforcement		
Design	**Results**	**Source**
This was an investigation of vouchers as incentives as a way to change behavior in cocaine users. Patients met with a therapist, received intensive case management, and had twice-a-week drug screens. One randomly assigned group also received vouchers for negative screens that increased in value with successive negative screens.	75% of the study subjects receiving vouchers completed the 12-week program compared to less than 50% of the control group. 60% of the voucher subjects remained abstinent at a 30-day follow-up compared to 45% for the control group. Incentives improved outcomes in outpatient behavioral treatment of cocaine dependence.	Higgins, S.T., Budney, A.J., Bickel, W.K., Foerg, F.E., and Donham, R. 1994. Incentives improve outcome in outpatient behavioral treatment of cocaine dependence. *Archives of General Psychiatry* 51:568–76.

Bibliography

American Dental Association. 2005. Dental topics A to Z: Methamphetamine use. Updated August 9, 2005. www.ada.org/prof/resources/topics/methmouth.asp.

Anglin, M. Douglas, Burke, Cynthia, Perrochet, Brian, Stamper, Ewa, and Dawud-Noursi, Samia. 2000. History of the methamphetamine problem. *Journal of Psychoactive Drugs* 32:137–41.

Anglin, M. Douglas, Hser, Yih-Ing, and Grella, Christine E. 1997. Drug addiction and treatment careers among clients in the drug abuse treatment study (DATOS). *Psychology of Addictive Behavior* 11:308–23.

Anglin, M. Douglas, and Rawson, Richard R. 1998. Center for Substance Abuse Treatment Replication of Effective Treatment Methamphetamine Dependence and Improvement of Cost-Effectiveness of Treatment Multi-Site Clinical Trial in Progress. Los Angeles, CA: University of California at Los Angeles.

Auerswald, Colette, and Eyre, Stephen L. 2002. Youth homelessness in San Francisco: A life cycle approach. *Social Science and Medicine* 54:1497–1512.

Bonné, Jon. 2001. Meth's deadly buzz. *MSNBC.COM Special Report.* http://msnbc.msn.com/id/3071772.

Brecht, Mary-Lynn. 2001. Update on methamphetamine use trends in California. Unpublished report. Los Angeles, CA: UCLA Integrated Substance Abuse Program.

Bungay, Vicky, Malchy, Leslie, Buxton, Jane A., Johnson, Joy, and MacPherson, Donald. 2006. Life with jib: A snapshot of street youth's use of crystal methamphetamine. *Addiction Research and Theory* 14 (3): 235–51.

Bureau of Justice Assistance. 2004. According to *Defining drug courts: The key components.* Washington, DC: Bureau of Justice. www.ojp.usdoj.gov/BJA/grant/drugcourts.html.

Bux, Donald A., Jr., and Irwin, Thomas W. 2006. Combining motivational interviewing and cognitive-behavioral skills training for the treatment of crystal methamphetamine abuse/dependence. *Journal of Gay and Lesbian Psychotherapy* 10 (3/4): 143–52.

Center for Substance Abuse Prevention/National Prevention Network. 2006. *Methamphetamine: A resource kit.* Rockville, MD: Substance Abuse and Mental Health Services Administration.

Cohen, Judith B., Dickow, Alice, Horner, Kathryn, Zweben, Joan E., Balabis, Jopseph, Vandersloot, Denna, and Reiber, Chris. 2003. Abuse and violence history of men and women in treatment for methamphetamine dependence. *The American Journal of Addictions* 12:377–85.

Correia, Christopher J., Sigmon, Stacey C., Silverman, Kenneth, Bigelow, George, and Stitzer, Maxine L. 2005. A comparison of voucher-delivery schedules for the initiation of cocaine abstinence. *Experimental and Clinical Psychopharmacology* 13 (3): 253–58.

Currie, Charles. 2005. Prevention and treatment on methamphetamine abuse. Testimony to the Senate Subcommittee on Labor, Health and Human Services, Education and Related Agencies Committee on Appropriations. April 21, 2005. www.hhs.gov/asl/testify/t050425.html.

Epstein, David H., Hawkins, Wesley E., Covi, Lino, Umbricht, Annie, and Preston, Kenzie L. 2003. Cognitive-behavioral therapy plus contingency management for cocaine use: Findings during treatment and across 12 month follow-up. *Psychology of Addictive Behaviors* 17 (1): 73–82.

Farrell, Michael, and Marsden, John. 2002. Editorial: Methamphetamine: Drug use and psychosis becomes a major public health issue in the Asia Pacific region. *Addiction* 97:771–72.

Freese, Thomas E., Obert, Jeanne, Dickow, Alice, Cohen, Judith B., and Lord, Russell H. 2000. Methamphetamine abuse: Issues for special populations. *Journal of Psychoactive Drugs* 32:177–82.

Gallant, Lewis E. 2006. Remarks provided to the Subcommittee on Criminal Justice, Drug Policy, and Human Resources, U.S. House of Representatives, Oversight Hearing on the National Synthetic Drug Control Strategy. June 16.

Gibson, David R., Leamon, Martin H., and Flynn, Neil. 2002. Epidemiology and public health consequences of methamphetamine use in California's central valley. *Journal of Psychoactive Drugs* 34:313–19.

Greenwell, Lisa, and Brecht, Mary-Lynn. 2003. Self-reported health status among treated methamphetamine users. *American Journal of Drug and Alcohol Abuse* 29 (1): 75–104.

Hanson, Glen R., Venturelli, Peter J., and Fleckenstein, Annette E. 2004. *Drugs and society.* 8th ed. Boston, MA: Jones and Bartlett.

Hendrickson, Robert G., Horowitz, B. Zane, Norton, Robert L., and Notenboom, Hans. 2006. "Parachuting" meth: A novel delivery method for methamphetamine and delayed-onset toxicity from "body stuffing." *Clinical Toxicology* 44:379–80.

Herz, Denise C. 2000. *Drugs in the heartland: Methamphetamine use in rural Nebraska.* The National Institute of Justice. Office of Justice Programs. April 2000. www.ncjrs.org/pdffiles1/nij/180986.pdf.

Higgins, Stephen T., Budney, Alan J., Bickel, Warren K., Foerg, Florian E., Donham, Robert, and Badger, Gary J. 1994. Incentives improve outcome in outpatient behavioral treatment of cocaine dependence. *Archives of General Psychiatry* 51:568–76.

Higgins, Stephen T., and Petry, Nancy M. 1999. Contingency management: Incentives for sobriety. *Alcohol Research & Health* 23 (2): 122–27.

Higgins, Stephen T., Sigmon, Stacey C., Wong, Conrad J., Heil, Sarah H., Badger, Gary J., Donham, Robert, Dantona, Robert L., and Anthony, Stacey. 2003. Community reinforcement therapy for cocaine dependent outpatients. *Archives of General Psychiatry* 60:1043–52.

Hohman, Melinda, Oliver, Rhonda, and Wright, Wendy. 2004. Methamphetamine abuse and manufacture: The child welfare response. *Social Work* 49 (3): 373–79.

Hser, Yih-Ing, Evans, Elizabeth, and Huang, Yu-Chuang. 2005. Treatment outcomes among women and men methamphetamine abusers in California. *Journal of Substance Abuse Treatment* 28:77–85.

Huber, Alice, Lord, Russell H., Gulati, Vikas, Marinelli-Casey, Patricia, Rawson, Richard A., and Ling, Walter. 2000. The CSAT methamphetamine treatment program: Research design accommodations for "real world" application. *Journal of Psychoactive Drugs* 32:149–56.

Huddleston, C. West, III. 2007. Drug courts: An effective strategy for communities facing methamphetamine. In *The methamphetamine crisis: Strategies to save addicts, families, and communities*, ed. Herbert C. Covey, 223–36. Westport, CT: Praeger.

Jang, Soo Mi, and Schoppelrey, Susan L. 2005. Implementation of contingency management substance abuse treatment in community settings. In *Addiction, assessment and treatment with adolescents, adults, and families*, ed. Carolyn Hilarski, 41–54. New York, NY: Haworth.

Joe, Karen. 1996. The lives and times of Asian-Pacific American women drug users: An ethnographic study of their methamphetamine use. *Journal of Drug Issues* 26 (1): 199–218.

Kall, K.I. 1992. Effects of amphetamine on sexual behavior of male IV drug users in Stockholm: A pilot study. *AIDS Education Prevention* 4:6–17.

Katsumata, Sumitoshi, Sato, K., and Kashiwade, H. 1993. Sudden death due presumably to internal use of methamphetamine. *Forensic Science* 62:209–15.

Kellogg, Scott H., Burns, Marylee, Coleman, Peter, Stitzer, Maxine, Wale, Joyce B., and Kreek, Mary Jeanne. 2005. Something of value: The introduction of contingency management interventions into the New York City Health and Hospital Addiction Treatment Service. *Journal of Substance Abuse Treatment* 28 (1): 57–65.

Kosten, Thomas, Poling, James, and Oliveto, Alison. 2003. Effects of reducing contingency management values on heroin and cocaine use for buprenorphine and desipramine-treated patients. *Addiction* 98 (5): 665–71.

Lee, Steven J. 2006. *Overcoming crystal meth addiction: An essential guide to getting clean.* New York, NY: Marlowe.

Leinwand, Donna. 2003. "Meth" moves east. *USA Today*, July 29.

Leshner, Alan I. 2000. Addressing the medical consequences of drug abuse. *NIDA Notes* 15:3–4.

Lewis, Marilyn W., and Petry, Nancy M. 2005. Contingency management treatments that reinforce completion of goal-related activities: Participation in family activities and its association with outcomes. *Drug and Alcohol Dependence* 79 (2): 267–71.

London, Edythe D., Simon, Sara L., Berman, Steven M., Mandelkern, Mark A., Lichtman, Aaron M., Bramen, Jennifer, Shinn, Ann K., et al. 2004. Mood disturbances and regional cerebral metabolic abnormalities in recently abstinent methamphetamine abusers. *Archives of General Psychiatry* 61:73–84.

Lovett, Anthony. 1994. Wired in California. *Rolling Stone* 681:39–40.

Marshall, Dane R. 2000. *Congressional Testimony to the Senate Judiciary Committee.* July 6.

Maslow, Abraham. 1943. A theory of human motivation. *Psychological Review* 50:370–96.

Messina, Nena, Marinelli-Casey, Patricia, West, Kathleen, and Rawson, Richard. 2007. Children exposed to methamphetamine use and manufacture. *Child Abuse and Neglect*, March 22.

Mills, Kimberly. 1999. Meth of old has morphed into epidemic proportions. *Seattle Post-Intelligencer*, December 13.

Molitor, Fred, Ruiz, Juan, Flynn, Neil, Mikanda, John, Sun, Richard K., and Anderson, Rachel. 1999. Methamphetamine use and sexual and injection risk behaviors among out-of-treatment injection drug users. *American Journal of Drug and Alcohol Abuse* 25 (3): 475–93.

Molitor, Fred, Truax, Steven R., Ruiz, Juan D., and Sun, Richard K. 1998. Association of methamphetamine use during sex with risky sexual behaviors and HIV infection among non-injecting drug users. *Western Journal of Medicine* 168 (2): 93–97.

Murr, Andrew. 2004. A new menace on the Rez. *Newsweek*, September 27, 30.

Nahom, Deborah. 2005. Motivational interviewing and behavior change: How can we know how it works? In *Addiction, assessment and treatment with adolescents, adults, and families*, ed. Carolyn Hilarski, 55–78. New York, NY: Haworth.

National Center on Addiction and Substance Abuse at Columbia University. 2000. *No place to hide: Substance abuse in mid-size cities and rural America.* New York, NY: Columbia University.

National Drug Intelligence Center. 2002. Crystal methamphetamine. *Information Bulletin*, August. Product Number 2002-L0424-005. Johnstown, PA: U.S. Department of Justice.

National Institute on Drug Abuse. 2002. *Research report: Methamphetamine abuse and addiction.* Bethesda, MD: National Institute on Drug Abuse.

———. 2005a. *Monitoring the future: National results of adolescent drug use.* Bethesda, MD: National Institute on Drug Abuse. http://www.monitoringthefuture.org/pubs.html.

———. 2005b. Medications development research for treatment of amphetamine and methamphetamine addiction—Report to Congress, August 2005. www.nida.nih.gov/about/legislation/MethReport/Efforts.html.

———. 2006. Developing effective addiction treatments. *NIDA Notes* 19 (1): 1–3. http://www.drugabuse.gov/NIDA_notes/NNvol19N1/Developing.html.

National Institutes of Health. 2001. Methamphetamine abuse leads to long-lasting changes in the human brain that are linked to impaired coordination and memory. *NIH News,* March 1. Washington, DC: U.S. Department of Health and Human Services. http://www.nih.gov/news/pr/mar2001/nida-01.htm.

———. 2004. New study suggests methamphetamine withdrawal is associated with brain changes similar to those seen in depression and anxiety. *NIH News,* January 5. Washington, DC: U.S. Department of Health and Human Services.

North Carolina Division of Social Services and the Family and Children's Resource Program. 2005. Methamphetamine: What child welfare workers should know. *Children's Services Practice Notes* 10 (2): April. http://info.dhhs.state.nc.us/olm/manuals/dss (accessed December 3, 2006).

O'Brien, Charles P., and McLellan, Thomas A. 1996. Myths about the treatment of addiction. *Lancet* 347:237–40.

Oetting, Eugene, Deffenbacher, Jerry, Taylor, Mathew, Luther, Nathan, Beauvais, Fred, and Edwards, Ruth. 2000. Methamphetamine use by high school students: Recent trends, gender, and ethnicity differences, and the use of other drugs. *Journal of Child and Adolescent Substance Abuse* 10 (1): 33–50.

Pennell, Susan, Ellett, Joe, Rienick, Cynthia, and Grimes, Jackie. 1999. *Meth matters; Report on methamphetamine users in five western cities.* Washington, DC: National Institute of Justice. http://ncjrs.org/pdffiles1/176331.pdf.

Petry, Nancy M., Alessi, Shelia M., Marx, Jacqueline, Austin, Mark, and Tardiff, Michelle. 2005. Vouchers versus prizes: Contingency management treatment of substance abusers in community settings. *Journal of Consulting and Clinical Psychology* 73 (6): 1005–14.

Petry, Nancy M., Martin, Bonnie, and Finocche, Charles. 2001. Contingency management in group treatment: A demonstration project in an HIV drop-in center. *Journal of Substance Abuse Treatment* 21:89–96.

Petry, Nancy M., Martin, Bonnie, and Simcic, Francis, Jr. 2005. Prize reinforcement contingency management for cocaine dependence: Integration with group therapy in a methadone clinic. *Journal of Consulting and Clinical Psychology* 72 (2): 354–59.

Petry, Nancy M., Peirce, Jessica M., Stitzer, Maxine L., Blaine, Jack, Roll, John M., Cohen, Allan, Obert, Jeanne, et al. 2005. Effect of prize-based incentives on outcomes in stimulant abusers in outpatient psychosocial treatment programs:

A national drug abuse treatment clinical trails network study. *Archives of General Psychiatry* 62 (10): 1148–56.

Petry, Nancy M., Tedford, Jacqueline, Austin, Mark, Nich, Charla, Carroll, Kathleen M., and Rounsaville, Bruce J. 2004. Prize reinforcement contingency management for treating cocaine users: How low can we go, and with whom? *Addiction* 99 (3): 349–60.

Poling, James, Oliveto, Alison, Petry, Nancy, Sofuoglu, Mehmet, Gonsai, Kishorchandra, Gonzales, Gerardo, Martell, Bridget, and Kosten, Thomas R. 2005. Six-month trial of bupropion with contingency management for cocaine dependence in a methadone-maintained population. *Archives of General Psychiatry* 63:219–28.

Prah, Pamela M. 2005. Methamphetamine. *CQ Researcher* 15 (25): 1–35.

Prochaska, J.D., DiClemente, C.C., and Norcross, J.C. 1992. In search of how people change: Applications to addictive behavior. *American Psychologist* 47:1102–14.

Rawson, Richard A. 2005. *Methamphetamine addiction: Cause for concern—Hope for the future.* Los Angeles, CA: Department of Psychiatry and Behavioral Sciences, UCLA. http://www2.apa.org/ppo/rawson62805.ppt.

Rawson, Richard A., Anglin, M. Douglas, and Ling, Walter. 2002. Will the methamphetamine problem go away? *Journal of Addictive Diseases* 21:5–19.

Rawson, Richard A., Huber, Alice, Brethen, Paul, Obert, Jeanne, Gulati, Vikas, Shoptaw, Steven, and Ling, Walter. 2000. Methamphetamine and cocaine users: Differences in characteristics and treatment retention. *Journal of Psychoactive Drugs* 32:233–38.

Rawson, Richard A., Huber, Alice, McCann, Michael, Shoptaw, Steven, Farabee, David, Reiber, Chris, and Ling, Walter. 2002. A comparison of contingency management and cognitive-behavioral approaches during methadone maintenance treatment for cocaine dependence. *Archives of General Psychiatry* 59:817–24.

Rawson, Richard A., Marinelli-Casey, Patricia J., Anglin, M. Douglas, Dickow, Alice, Frazier, Yvonne, Gallagher, Cheryl, Galloway, Gantt P., et al. 2004. A multi-site comparison of psychosocial approaches for the treatment of methamphetamine dependence. *Addiction* 99:708–17.

Rawson, Richard A., McCann, Michael J., Flammino, Frank, Shoptaw, Steven, Miotto, Karen, Reiber, Chris, and Ling, Walter. 2006. A comparison of contingency management and cognitive-behavioral approaches for stimulant-dependent individuals. *Addiction* 101 (2): 267–74.

Reback, Cathy J., and Grella, Christine E. 1999. HIV risk behaviors of gay and bisexual male methamphetamine users contacted through street outreach. *Journal of Drug Issues* 29 (1): 35–44.

Rodriguez, Nancy, Katz, Charles, Webb, Vincent J., and Schaefer, David R. 2005. Examining the impact of individual, community, and market factors on methamphetamine use: A tale of two cities. *Journal of Drug Issues* 22:665–94.

Roll, John M., Huber, Alice, Sodano, Ruthlyn, Chudzynski, Joy E., Moynier, Eugene, and Shoptaw, Steven. 2006. A comparison of five reinforcement schedules for use in contingency management based treatment of methamphetamine abuse. *The Psychological Record* 56 (1): 67–81.

Roll, John M., Petry, Nancy M., Brecht, Mary L., Peirce, Jessica M., McCann, Michael J., Blaine, Jack, Macdonald, Marilyn, Dimaria, Joan, Lucero, Leroy, and Kellogg, Scott. 2006. Contingency management for the treatment of methamphetamine use disorders. *American Journal of Psychiatry* 163 (11): 1993–99.

Rowan-Szal, Grace A., Bartholomew, Norma G., Chatham, Lois R., and Simpson, Dwayne D. 2005. A combined behavioral intervention for cocaine-using methadone clients. *Journal of Psychoactive Drugs* 37 (1): 75–84.

Shoptaw, Steven, Jarvik, Murray E., Ling, Walter, Rawson, Richard A. 1996. Contingency management for tobacco smoking in methadone-maintained opiate addicts. *Addictive Behavior* 21 (3): 409–12.

Shoptaw, Steven, Reback, Cathy J., Peck, Janet A., Yang, Xiaowei, Rotheram-Fuller, Erin, Larkins, Sherry, Veniegas, Rosemary C., Freese, Thomas E., and Hucks-Ortiz, Christopher. 2005. Behavioral treatment approaches for methamphetamine dependence and HIV-related sexual risk behaviors among urban gay and bisexual men. *Drug and Alcohol Dependence* 78 (2): 125–34.

Sigmon, Stacey C., Correia, Christopher J., and Stitzer, Maxine L. 2004. Cocaine abstinence during methadone maintenance: Effects of repeated brief exposure to voucher-based reinforcement. *Experimental and Clinical Psychopharmacology* 12 (4): 269–75.

Simon, Sara L., Richardson, Kimberly, Dacey, Jennifer, Glynn, Susan, Domier, Catherine P., Rawson, Richard A., and Ling, Walter. 2002. A comparison of patterns of methamphetamine and cocaine use. *Journal of Addictive Disease* 21 (1): 35–44.

Singer, Merrill, Mirhej, Greg, Santelices, Claudia, Hastings, Erica, Navarro, Juhem, and Vivian, Jim. 2006. Tomorrow is already here, or is it? Steps in preventing a local methamphetamine outbreak. *Human Organization* 65 (2): 203–18.

Sommers, Ira, Baskin, Deborah, and Baskin-Sommers, Arielle. 2006. Methamphetamine use among young adults: Health and social consequences. *Addictive Behaviors* 31 (8): 1469–76.

Spoth, Richard L., Clair, Scott, Shin, Chungyeol, and Redmond, Cleve. 2006. Long-term effects of universal preventive interventions on methamphetamine use among adolescents. *Archives of Pediatrics and Adolescent Medicine* 160:876–82.

Substance Abuse and Mental Health Services Administration (SAMHSA). 2001. *Summary of Findings 2000 National Household Survey on Drug Abuse.* Rockville, MD: SAMHSA.

———. 2004. Primary methamphetamine/amphetamine treatment admissions: 1992–2002. *The DASIS Report* September 17, 2004. Rockville, MD: SAMHSA.

———. 2005a. *National Survey on Drug Use and Health 2004.* Updated October 2, 2005. Rockville, MD: SAMHSA.

———. 2005b. *The NSDUH Report: Methamphetamine Use, Abuse, and Dependence: 2002, 2003, and 2004, In Brief.* Updated September 16, 2005. Rockville, MD: SAMHSA.

————. 2005c. Smoked methamphetamine/amphetamines: 1992–2002. *The DASIS Report* January 7. Rockville, MD: SAMHSA.

————. 2006. Trends in methamphetamine/amphetamine admissions to treatment: 1993–2003. *The DASIS Report* March 15.

United Nations Office for Drug Control and Crime Prevention. 2006. *World Drug Report.* New York, NY: Oxford University Press.

Volkow, Nora D. 2006. Testimony before the Subcommittee on Criminal Justice, Drug Policy, and Human Resources, Committee on Government Reform, United States House of Representatives. June 28.

Volkow, Nora D., Chang, Linda, Wang, Gene-Jack, Fowler, Joanna S., Franceschi, Dinko, Sedler, Mark J., Gatley, S. John, et al. 2001b. Higher cortical and lower subcortical metabolism in detoxified methamphetamine abusers. *The American Journal of Psychiatry* 158:383–89.

Volkow, Nora D., Chang, Linda, Wang, Gene-Jack, Fowler, Joanna S., Leonido-Yee, Maria, Franceschi, Dinko, Sedler, Mark J., et al. 2001a. Association of dopamine transporter reduction with psychomotor impairment in methamphetamine abusers. *The American Journal of Psychiatry* 158 (3): 377–82.

Wells, Kathryn. 2006. *The Methamphetamine crisis,* ed. H.C. Covey. Westport, CT: Praeger.

Wermuth, Laurie. 2000. Methamphetamine use: Hazards and social influences. *Journal of Drug Education* 30:423–33.

Whitten, Lori. 2006. Treatment curbs methamphetamine abuse among gay and bisexual men. *NIDA Notes* 20 (4): 4–5.

Yacoubian, George S., and Peters, Ronald J. 2004. Exploring the prevalence and correlates of methamphetamine use: Findings from Sacramento's ADAM program. *Journal of Drug Education* 34:281–94.

Zickler, Patrick. 2005a. Methamphetamine, cocaine abusers have different patterns of drug use, suffer cognitive impairments. *NIDA Notes* 16:1–2.

————. 2005b. Ethnic identification and cultural ties may help prevent drug use. *NIDA Notes* 14:1–3.

Zule, William A., and Desmond, David P. 1999. An ethnographic comparison of HIV risk behaviors among heroin and methamphetamine injectors. *American Journal of Drug and Alcohol Abuse* 25 (1): 1–23.

Index

depression, 15, 34–35, 37, 45, 48, 50–
  51, 55–58, 60, 71–72, 85
domains, 26–27, 88–90; biological, 26–
  27, 88–90; psychological, 26–28, 38–
  39; social, 26–27, 42, 88–90
dopamine, 28, 30, 32, 33
Desoxyn, 47
drug court, 93–96, 114–16, 126, 128–
  29, 144–45, 155–56
drug testing, 93, 97–98, 114–15, 134

Edeleano, L., 45
effects: biological, 27, 32; distal, 35–36;
  implications for treatment, 52–55;
  long-term, 49–52; proximal, 35–36;
  psychological, 32, 54; short-term,
  49–52; social, 42–43
engagement, 152–54
enmeshment, 45, 51
epinephrine, 28, 30
expectations: about methamphetamine,
  53, 86, 88, 104, 107, 124, 125, 131,
  134–42, 154, 158–59

family-based interventions, 155–59
female use, 3, 44–45, 55, 59–60

hierarchy of needs, 56, 90–92
hippocampus, 33–34
human immunodeficiency virus (HIV),
  57, 73

identification, 150
infectious diseases, 51, 57, 73

lobes: frontal, 33–34; parietal, 33–34;
  temporal, 33

male use, 3, 54, 58, 60
Maslow, Abraham, 90–91
Matrix model, 68, 70, 72–73
medications, 55, 68, 71
methamphetamine: epidemic, 1–5;
  expectations of, 86–87, 104, 107, 112,
  124–25, 135–42, 154, 158–59; history
  of, 2–3, 45–46; lifestyle, 1, 2, 26, 35–
  37, 44, 73, 83, 90, 93, 98–99, 117,

124–25, 127–28; pleasure derived
  from, 39; sex, 45, 61; understanding
  use, 25; uniqueness of, 26, 52; use in
  rural areas, 53, 60–61
Methamphetamine Control Act of
  1996, 46
methamphetamine-using community,
  22–23, 25, 41–42, 52–53, 112;
  avoidance of, 84–85
Montana Meth Project, 41–42
motivational enhancement therapy
  (MET), 70
motivational incentives for enhancing
  drug abuse recovery, 70
motivational interviewing (MI), 71–72

Native Americans, 61–62
neurons, 27–33; effects of
  methamphetamine on, 31–32
neuroreceptors, 28
neurotoxicity, 31–32
neurotransmitters, 27–32
norepinephrine, 29, 30
nucleus accumbens, 32–33

Ogata, Akira, 46
Olds, James, 32
operant conditioning, 34–37, 41

paranoia, 43, 48, 54–55
pleasure, 40–41
post-traumatic stress disorder (PTSD),
  55, 104
prefrontal cortex, 33
prevalence, 4, 62–67; DAWN (Drug
  Abuse Warning Network), 64–65;
  MTF (Monitoring the Future), 62–
  65; National Household Survey on
  Drug Abuse, 66–67; reports on,
  DASIS (Drug and Alcohol Services
  Information System), 59, 66; TEDS
  (Treatment Episode Data System),
  56, 64–66
prevention, 4, 6, 41, 48, 54, 62, 68, 70,
  82, 149–50, 159–60

recalibration, 6, 143–46

About the Authors

NICOLAS T. TAYLOR is a Licensed Clinical Psychologist and Certified Addictions Counselor, practicing in the rural areas of western Colorado. A member of the Colorado state methamphetamine task force, he is also Treatment Workgroup Chair for the National Alliance for Drug Endangered Children. His earlier roles have included facilitating therapy groups for inmates/substance abusers at Utah State Prison and teaching at the West Slope CASA Addictions Counselor Certification Training Consortium, as well as Mesa State College. A nationally recognized expert on methamphetamine treatment, he has also been an instructor at Brigham Young University and has presented talks as well as training sessions at the Colorado Department of Human Services Methamphetamine Symposium, the annual Drug Endangered Children Conference in Washington, D.C., and the Indian Health Services Annual Behavioral Health Conference.

HERBERT C. COVEY is the Deputy Director of the Adams County Social Services Department in Colorado and part-time instructor at the University of Colorado at Boulder. He received his Ph.D. in Sociology from the University of Colorado. He has written numerous academic books and articles and is the editor of *The Methamphetamine Crisis* (Praeger, 2006).